MW01469720

Energy Almanac

52 Weekly Astrology Predictions & Holistic Resources
A Journal for 2025

Veilleux, Tam | Energy Almanac, 2024-2025

LUMINOUS
MOON
PRESS
BOULDER, COLORADO

Published by Luminous Moon Press, LLC
Edited by Michelle Schweitzer, Chelyn Consulting
Design by Carolyn Oakley, www.luminousmoon.com
Cover Art by Tam Veilleux, 2024

ISBN-13: 979-8-9916548-0-7

https://luminousmoon.com
https://choosebigchange.com

Energy Almanac 2025 Edition

✡ https://choosebigchange.com ✡

"Whatever lifts the corners of your mouth, trust that."

-Rumi

FROM THE CREATOR OF
Energy Almanac

——— ◇◆◇ ———

Dear Reader,

It's hard to believe that you're holding book seven in what I supposed back in 2018 would be a short run of writing an annual astrology publication. What a surprise and delight it is to bring you the 2025 Energy Almanac. As I was writing the predictions this year, I noticed some very clear themes. It started with the number 9, the sum of the numbers 2025. "Oh! A year of closure" I said to myself. Nines represent the end of a cycle of sorts. When you think logically about a season in your life and the closing of a cycle, you immediately understand that you have gained wisdom. You are now the crone with insights to share. As that was simmering in my subconscious and I pecked away at my keyboard, leadership lessons (Neptune and Saturn in Aries) and ancestral wisdom (Jupiter in Cancer) kept coming at me along with intuition and imagination.

It seems to me the message is clear. We are working on pulling out the bits of wisdom gained from strife and learning how to live together from a place of individuality. The key is in service to the whole in mind. It's as though you've played with a recipe over the last 8 years, and now you know what makes the cake taste good or bad. Those bits of wisdom can be applied as you move forward in 2025.

Your individual work is to listen more often to your intuitive knowledge and apply it to your life as a leader. You don't have to be the CEO of a business, you have to be the CEO of your own life. Lead with and from the heart. It has all the intuition you need. If I were to suggest one useful tool for 2025, it's this: Ask and listen. Ask your gut, your higher self or your angel, "Will this serve me and the greater good? What do I do next?" Applied intuition is the name of the game. Well, that and heart-centered leadership.

I am excited to introduce you to new resource sections this year. Rhythms, Routines & Rituals will help you break old habits and develop new soul-fueled practices while the Wisdom Diaries are story-style lessons in grace and growth. Human Design is here to stay. I know you'll enjoy the Gift & Shadow section again this year. Numerology is woven into monthly overview articles. Gemstones and essential oils are readily available and this year there is a place for you to play with your favorite oracle deck and a monthly calendar in case you wanted to use your Energy Almanac for planning. Also new this year you'll notice more lines for writing. Each weekly prediction is followed by lines

Energy Almanac 2025 EDITION

✵ https://choosebigchange.com ✵

Copyright © 2024-2025 Tam Veilleux. All rights reserved worldwide.

for you to capture thoughts either before the week starts or after the week is over.

I believe autumn is the season to watch in 2025 with yods, kites and trines galore. I'd suggest you have your spiritual practices in place to reinforce your stability.

As always, it's a delight to serve you. Enjoy practicing weaving wisdom into all of your days.

To the year ahead!

TAM VEILLEUX ♍
Artist/Alchemist/Astro-Junkie

NOTE TO READER: All dates and times throughout Energy Almanac are in UTC Coordinated Universal Time (American/New York). Reference materials include Astro.com, CafeAstrology.com, and The American Ephemeris for the 21st Century, Neil Michelsen and Rique Pottenger, January 15, 2010. We thank you for allowing for human error. This publication goes through many sets of eyes, all of which are human. In between coffee spills, chocolate smears on our computer screens, exhaustion and glee, mistakes can be made. We are grateful for your softness in witnessing and dismissing small mistakes.

PLEASE VISIT OUR ONLINE SHOP FOR THE HOLISTIC RESOURCES YOU NEED FOR 2025.
HTTPS://CHOOSEBIGCHANGE.COM

RESOURCES FOR YOUR JOURNEY

HOW TO USE YOUR
Energy Almanac

LEAVE IT IN A CONSPICUOUS LOCATION

- Be sure you leave the book where you'll see it often.
- Each week's astrology reads Monday through Sunday.

READ AND RE-READ

- Read the book all the way through one time, highlighting pieces of information that intrigue you or may be relevant according to date.

- Read a second time with a notebook nearby—purposefully read and list information relevant to your life and profession.

- Note key dates or themes i.e. moons, retrogrades, or choice points in the month-at-a-glance calendar we've provided for easy reference. Get creative!

- Set a weekly reminder on your phone so you never forget to check the astrological prediction for the week ahead.

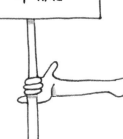

ORDER ALL OF THE MONTHLY HOLISTIC RESOURCES AHEAD OF TIME

✧ https://choosebigchange.com ✧

How the Planets Play

PLANETS

Recall, if you will, the Roman myths we learned. Think of the ten planets as actors from those tales. Each planet is named after a character in a story with its own personality and traits. For example, in mythology, Saturn was the god of time and taught agriculture to his people. Saturn rules time, karma, discipline, and responsibility.

ZODIAC SIGNS

Consider the twelve zodiac signs as pieces of clothing that the planets might wear for a period of time. Each sign has specific qualities, traits, strengths, weaknesses, and general attitudes toward life. When a planet is traversing in any specific sign, its personality will be affected by the qualities of the sign. Example: The zodiac sign of Virgo is known for being analytical, health-oriented, mentally astute, detailed, preachy, overwhelmed, self-critical, and uptight.

ASTROLOGICAL HOUSES

The twelve houses of astrology represent where the character of the story will be. It's the stage or scene they will act in. The houses range from internal areas such as values, wishes and goals, shadow work, or identity to more external and tangible areas such as children, money, religion, and career. As a planet moves through a house, that area of life will feel the pressure of said planet.

ASPECTS

Aspects speak to how exactly the characters will play together based on where they are located. Maybe they'll be kind to one another (conjunct), or maybe someone will take their ball and go home (opposition). Some aspects create ease (conjunct, sextile) while others create discord (square, Grand Cross) and tension. Aspects are neither good nor bad. They simply show the relationship between planets.

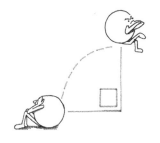

Energy Almanac 2025 Edition

♡ Love the Energy Almanac? Tag us on social media: @TheEnergyAlmanac ♡

Page 7

Planets

Think of the ten planets as actors. Each planet is a character in a story, each with its own personality and traits indicating what the character/planet must do.

SUN

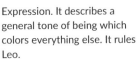 Expression. It describes a general tone of being which colors everything else. It rules Leo.

MOON

 Emotion. It represents our feelings and emotions, the receptivity, intuition, imagination, and basic feeling tone of a person. It also affects our sense of rhythm and time. It rules Cancer.

MERCURY

Communication. It represents reason, common sense, analyzing, data collection and the process of learning and skills. It rules Gemini and Virgo.

VENUS

 Relations. It gives us a sense of pleasure, aesthetic awareness, love of harmony, sociability, partnership, and eroticism. It rules Libra and Taurus.

MARS

 Action. It represents the energy and drive of a person; courage, determination, the freedom of spontaneous impulse. It also describes the readiness for action, the way one goes about doing things, and simple aggression. It rules Aries.

JUPITER

 Expansion. It represents the search for individual meaning and purpose, optimism, hope, and a sense of justice, along with faith, a basic philosophy of life, wealth, religion, spiritual growth. It rules Sagittarius.

SATURN

 Limitation. It shows how we experience "reality," where we meet with resistance and discover our limitations, moral convictions, and structure. It lends qualities like earnestness, caution, and reserve. It rules Capricorn.

URANUS

 Revelation. It represents intuition, originality, independence, and an openness for all that is new, unknown, and unusual. It creates a shift in thinking. It rules Aquarius.

NEPTUNE

 Compassion. It represents the mysterious and supersensory, mystical experience, and is creative, intuitive, and imaginative. Watch for deception, illusion, and false appearances as well as escapism in all its forms. It rules Pisces.

PLUTO

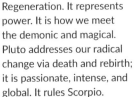 Regeneration. It represents power. It is how we meet the demonic and magical. Pluto addresses our radical change via death and rebirth; it is passionate, intense, and global. It rules Scorpio.

THIS INFORMATION IS NOW AVAILABLE AS AN ONLINE CLASS.
Go to www.choosebigchange.com/products/sync-thrive-class

 https://choosebigchange.com

Zodiac Signs

◇◇◇

Each zodiac sign carries specific tendencies and traits. Think of them as a costume that the planet pulls on as it progresses through the sign. The costume indicates how the planet will behave.

ARIES

MARCH 21-APRIL 19

Fire. Ruled by Mars. Brave, Direct, Fearless, Bold, Independent, Natural born leaders. Aggressive, Pushy, Selfish, Inconsistent. Think: Football uniform

TAURUS

APRIL 20-MAY 20

Earth. Ruled by Venus. Steady, Loyal, Tenacious, Trustworthy, Patient. Resistant to change, Stubborn, Materialistic, Indulgent. Think: Denim overalls

GEMINI

MAY 21-JUNE 20

Air. Ruled by Mercury. Intelligent, Adaptable, Communicative, Agile, Socially connected. Talkative, Superficial, Cunning, Exaggerating. Think: Color-blocked shirt

CANCER

JUNE 21-JULY 22

Water. Ruled by the Moon. Nurturing, Supportive, Compassionate, Loving, Healing. Dependent, Indirect, Moody, Passive-aggressive, Holds on too long. Think: Fluffy bathrobe

LEO

JULY 23-AUG 22

Fire. Ruled by the Sun. Brave, Generous, Charismatic, Fun, Playful, Warm, Protective. Egotistical, Controlling, Drama King/Queen, Dominating, Shows off. Think: Sundress and microphone

VIRGO

AUG 23-SEPT 22

Earth. Ruled by Mercury. Modest, Orderly, Practical, Down-to-earth, Logical, Altruistic, Organized. Obsessive, Perfectionist, Critical, Overly analytical. Think: Medical lab coat

LIBRA

SEPT 23-OCT 22

Air. Ruled by Venus. Charming, Diplomatic, Polished, Sweet-natured, Social. Indecisive, Superficial, Out of balance, Gullible, People pleasing. Think: Sequined dress, diamonds, and a scale

SCORPIO

OCT 23-NOV 21

Water. Ruled by Mars and Pluto. Passionate, Driven, Perceptive, Determined, Sacrificing, Emotional Depth. Vindictive, Jealous, Paranoid, Destructive, Possessive, Passive-aggressive. Think: Black hoodie

SAGITTARIUS

NOV 22-DEC 21

Fire. Ruled by Jupiter. Ambitious, Lucky, Optimistic, Enthusiastic, Open-minded, Moral. Restless, Blunt, Irresponsible, Tactless, Lazy, Overly indulgent. Think: Logo T-shirt and backpack

CAPRICORN

DEC 22-JAN 19

Earth. Ruled by Saturn. Driven, Disciplined, Responsible, Persistent, Business-minded. Pessimistic, Greedy, Cynical, Rigid, Miserly, Ruthless. Think: Three-piece suit

AQUARIUS

JAN 20-FEB 18

Air. Ruled by Saturn and Uranus. Intelligent, Inventive, Humanitarian, Friendly, Reformative. Emotionally detached, Impersonal, Scattered, Non-committal. Think: Astronaut outfit

PISCES

FEB 19-MARCH 20

Water. Ruled by Neptune. Mystical, Intuitive, Compassionate, Romantic, Creative, Sensitive. Escapist, Victims, Codependent, Unrealistic, Submissive, Dependent. Think: Artists' smock

Energy Almanac 2025 Edition

The Astrological Houses

All western astrology charts are divided into 12 sections called houses. Each house represents an area of life. When you find a planet in a specific house it will show you which domain will be affected. Remember that the planets have a job that indicates WHAT their role is, or what they are doing. The zodiac costume is HOW they might behave while in that role. The house indicates WHERE in your life this is playing out.

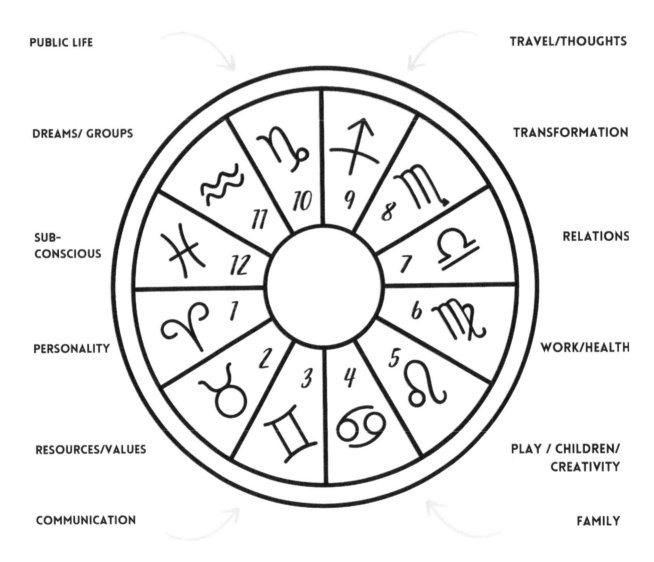

PUBLIC LIFE

TRAVEL/THOUGHTS

DREAMS/ GROUPS

TRANSFORMATION

SUB-CONSCIOUS

RELATIONS

PERSONALITY

WORK/HEALTH

RESOURCES/VALUES

PLAY / CHILDREN/ CREATIVITY

COMMUNICATION

FAMILY

2025 Energy Sketch

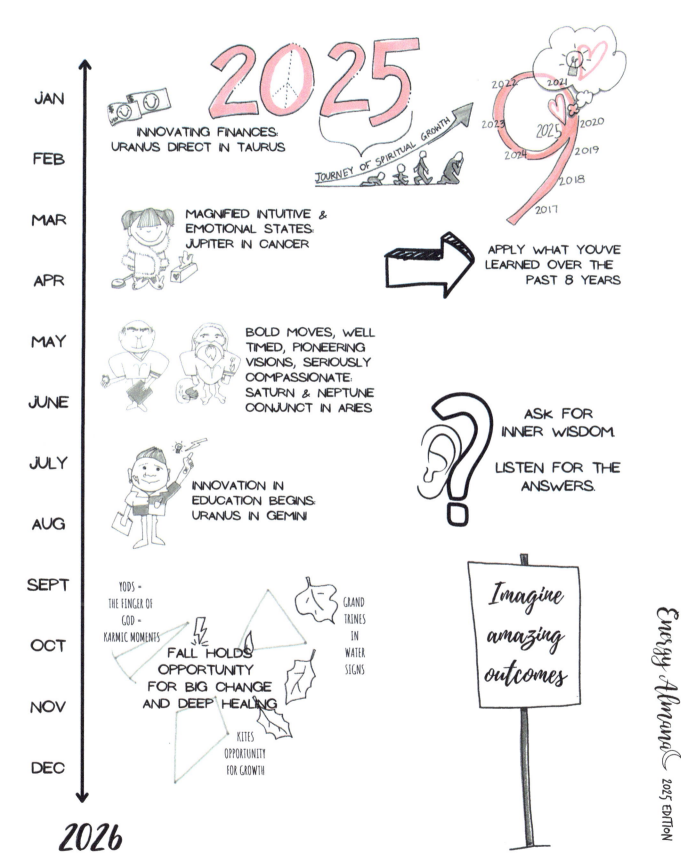

JAN

INNOVATING FINANCES:
URANUS DIRECT IN TAURUS

2025

JOURNEY OF SPIRITUAL GROWTH

2022 2021
2023   2020
      2025
2024   2019
       2018
    2017

FEB

MAR

MAGNIFIED INTUITIVE &
EMOTIONAL STATES:
JUPITER IN CANCER

APPLY WHAT YOU'VE
LEARNED OVER THE
PAST 8 YEARS

APR

MAY

BOLD MOVES, WELL
TIMED, PIONEERING
VISIONS, SERIOUSLY
COMPASSIONATE:
SATURN & NEPTUNE
CONJUNCT IN ARIES

JUNE

ASK FOR
INNER WISDOM.

LISTEN FOR THE
ANSWERS.

JULY

INNOVATION IN
EDUCATION BEGINS:
URANUS IN GEMINI

AUG

SEPT

YODS =
THE FINGER OF
GOD =
KARMIC MOMENTS

GRAND
TRINES
IN
WATER
SIGNS

Imagine
amazing
outcomes

OCT

FALL HOLDS
OPPORTUNITY
FOR BIG CHANGE
AND DEEP HEALING

NOV

KITES
OPPORTUNITY
FOR GROWTH

DEC

2026

Energy Almanac 2025 EDITION

Important Planetary Moves

The large outer planets play an interesting and effective role in the psyches of the masses. Their influence on human behavior can often be witnessed in the evening news. In order to understand what the mundane world might experience due to planetary placements we must look to Pluto, Uranus, Neptune, Jupiter, and Saturn individually. Each of these planets have their own role depending on which zodiac costume they are wearing. Let's take a look at the characters for the year ahead.

PLUTO IN AQUARIUS
(RETROGRADE IN AQUARIUS MAY 4 – OCTOBER 13)

Still in its earliest degrees, Pluto in Aquarius brings about the foreshadowing of the rebuilding of society. Pluto, if you think of him as the Tasmanian Devil, will take down and deconstruct old ideas about how we care for the group, freedom, innovation and intuition and force society to find new ways of handling all of those ideas. Since Aquarius is futuristic and is the manager of "invisible waves", it's likely that there will be some new ways of using technology and even frequencies. Let's look for technology that heals us. Watch for the impact of AI on our world in a way that is benevolent. Innovation is on high for the next 20 years. Use retrograde seasons to ask "How well are we handling the transformation of Aquarian topics?"

NEPTUNE IN PISCES AND ARIES
(RETROGRADE IN ARIES SEPTEMBER 1 THEN RETROGRADE IN PISCES OCTOBER 23)

The placement of Neptune in Pisces has been heightening spirituality, intuition, and creativity as well as compassion. It's been a long season of amplifying your inner world with ritual, prayer, sound, journaling, and impassioned intention setting. Hopefully humanity is now listening to the benevolent voices within as part of a daily practice. With amplified faith in the unseen tied up securely in a lovely bow, we can now trust in knowing miracles are available to you if you will have them. The long transit through Pisces ends in March when the ideological water-bearing planet enters the fiery zodiac of Aries creating a wealth of steam.

We have a faith-filled and compassionate grandfather character, Neptune himself, pulling on the football uniform of Aries on March 30. Imagine this! An ideological and imaginative grandfather in a football uniform ready to take impassioned action. This twenty-plus year transit will build out leaders who are unique, and hopefully compassionate, in their boldness. We could see a dynamic change in humans willing to stand up and be seen, take risks within their own worlds. Will Neptune temper the typically passionate nature of Aries and bring forth the quiet strength of loving leaders for an entire generation or will the warring nature of the Roman athlete win? Focus with intention on which angle would produce better results. Aries can be impulsive and rash, let's lean into the compassion of Neptune for the win.

Neptune will retrograde in both signs beginning in September. This is the chance to see how leadership feels with spirituality attached and it's a second opportunity to reflect on how your spiritual practices have developed. In early January 2026 Neptune will don the Aries costume and stay there for a twelve-year journey.

Energy Almanac 2025 Edition

✳ https://choosebigchange.com ✳

URANUS IN TAURUS AND GEMINI
(RETROGRADE IN TAURUS UNTIL JANUARY 29, RETROGRADE AGAIN SEPTEMBER 6)

The planet of revelation, Uranus, will be retrograde in the steady sign of Taurus as the year opens. Change is in the air when this planet spends its time in the zodiac of our resources and self-worth. Its main desire is to shift slow-moving society into new ways with money and resources as well as value systems. We'll do some deep thinking about the innovations inside of the broader economy before Uranus begins its long tour in the color-blocked buttoned up shirt of Gemini. Refer to the astrology primer on pages 8-9.

On July 8, Uranus changes its sign. Gemini is curious and social. The higher mind of Uranus is going to do a dance with the frontal lobe of society for the next many years. Gemini, in the mundane world, addresses our education system and learning as well as social networks. Innovating these areas will begin and big questions will lead to big answers as revelation after revelation occurs. What unique possibilities will we explore about how we teach and learn? The next seven years may find us asking, "Who knew?!" and then using AI for the answer.

SATURN IN PISCES AND ARIES
(RETROGRADE JULY 13 – NOVEMBER 27)

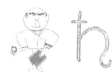

The "cosmic thumb" of the cosmos, Saturn, is the bringer of lessons. He expects discipline, integrity, and responsibility as well as a tight grip on timing. When wearing the flowing artists' smock of Pisces, Saturn offers us a taste of "magical realism"—the opportunity to dream it and then put a foundation under it. While Saturn creates limits, the big dreamer Pisces is limitless in its expectations. This transit involves dissolving boundaries (self-imposed or otherwise) and rethinking habits while developing spiritual practices. It's time to take your spirituality seriously, Little Pretzel.

In May of 2025, Saturn will enter Aries, the zodiac represented by the football uniform. Here we have responsible leadership, right timing of actions, repressed or responsible boldness and lessons inside of our individuality. It will be interesting to see how the seriousness of Saturn is applied to individuals. A general slowing of action-taking could occur which will allow for a more planned approach to life.

JUPITER IN GEMINI AND CANCER
(JUNE 9, 2025 AND JUNE 30, 2026)

When Jupiter, our cosmic cheerleader, is wearing the Gemini color-blocked button-down shirt with a pocket protector in place, you know that curiosity is high. This set-up is designed to help society develop new ideas around education and expanded learning. It's also a highly social time and the urge to gather may be present, too. If you haven't already, do buy yourself a bunch of notebooks as Gemini loves communication and data. The year opens with Jupiter in retrograde. As your questions arise and answers follow, capture all of it in your notebook.

Jupiter moves into the sign of Cancer on June 10th. Imagine the ever-optimistic cheerleader in her fluffy pink housecoat and bunny slippers. Here we have an expanded intuition and the desire to nurture each other over the coming months. Think of home gatherings, dining together at the family dining table and caring for each other. The sign of the crab taps deeply into family while Jupiter is about our wisdom. What ancestral wisdom can we tap into and share under this transit? Cancer is naturally emotional, too. Be wary of having your heart on your sleeve or claws out as the sign of the crab may put a pinch on relationships if you aren't careful. Cocooning is another potential. Don't forget to add play dates to your calendar so that you actually leave home. This societal pattern will hold for the rest of 2025 and into May of 2026.

VISIT OUR ONLINE STORE FOR JOURNALS THAT WILL SUPPORT YOUR 2025 JOURNEY
HTTPS://CHOOSEBIGCHANGE.COM

♡ Love the Energy Almanac? Tag us on social media: @TheEnergyAlmanac ♡

Energy Almanac 2025 Edition

Page 13

Marvelous Moon Work

The two luminaries, sun and moon, are probably the most watched of all of the celestial bodies. Walking outside to witness their glory can be breathtaking. To understand the fullness of what they represent when wearing specific zodiacs is a whole other level of participating in creating your own reality.

This year's moon articles were written with a coaching perspective. The goal is to engage yourself in a way that will have you working with the energies at hand so that you can grow from each experience.

Each month holds an explanation of which planets are being aspected along with some insight as to the potentials that will be created. This is followed by an affirmation for you to use as well as three exercises that could generate new thoughts under the influence of the moons. All of the exercises are for you to accept or reject based on your own intuitive responses.

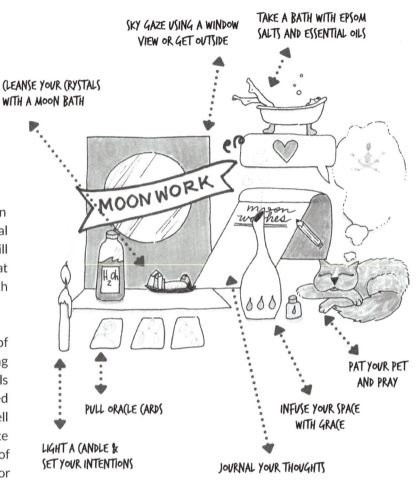

SKY GAZE USING A WINDOW VIEW OR GET OUTSIDE

TAKE A BATH WITH EPSOM SALTS AND ESSENTIAL OILS

CLEANSE YOUR CRYSTALS WITH A MOON BATH

MOON WORK

PULL ORACLE CARDS

PAT YOUR PET AND PRAY

INFUSE YOUR SPACE WITH GRACE

LIGHT A CANDLE & SET YOUR INTENTIONS

JOURNAL YOUR THOUGHTS

You are encouraged to read and choose to do what feels best for you. No matter which exercises you employ, be sure you keep a journal of how the moon is affecting you this year. The patterns that are reflected can inform your future. And that is worth its weight in gold.

Moon articles written by Tam Veilleux, artist, alchemist, astrology-junkie
www.choosebigchange.com | IG @TheEnergyAlmanac

✵ https://choosebigchange.com ✵

A Note About Eclipses

◇❖◇

Each year, at least two of the New and Full Moons are also a Solar or Lunar Eclipse. These dynamic events take place when the sun, earth, and moon align so that the new moon will cover the face of the sun from the earth's perspective—creating the solar eclipse, or the earth will block the sun's light from reaching the full moon—bringing the lunar eclipse.

An Eclipse indicates a major change will arrive. It has a 6-month influence and can be felt as far as 6 weeks before it occurs. The Solar Eclipse is about identity and marks a change in an outer world circumstance; the Lunar Eclipse is about feelings and marks a change in relationships. Avoid beginning new ventures on or during the week before and after an eclipse.

All times throughout the Almanac are UTC Coordinated Universal Time (American/New York)

WILD CARDS

SOLAR · LUNAR

POWERFUL THINGS CAN HAPPEN

A WAVE OF ENERGY BRINGING ABOUT new awareness, shifts & healing

SOMETHING WILL CHANGE

2025 ECLIPSES

MARCH 14, 2:54 AM
FULL MOON TOTAL LUNAR ECLIPSE AT 23° VIRGO

MARCH 29, 6:58 AM
NEW MOON PARTIAL SOLAR ECLIPSE AT 9° ARIES

SEPTEMBER 7, 2:09 PM
FULL MOON TOTAL LUNAR ECLIPSE AT 15° PISCES

SEPTEMBER 21, 3:54 PM
NEW MOON PARTIAL SOLAR ECLIPSE AT 29° VIRGO

♡ Love the Energy Almanac? Tag us on social media: @TheEnergyAlmanac ♡

The Lunar Nodes

◇ ◆ ◇

PISCES – VIRGO: PRACTICAL SPIRITUALITY

The two Lunar Nodes are a specific moving point in space where the Sun and Moon's orbital paths around the Earth intersect. Unlike the planets, the Moon's nodes move in a clockwise direction—Taurus toward Aries, for example—around the zodiac. The north node represents the way forward or karmic destiny; it is considered as Jupiter, a point where benefits are found. It represents a positive evolutionary direction, what we need to learn, our cosmic mission so to speak. The South Node is considered as Saturn, or karmic history and lessons, a point of constriction. It represents old instincts that must be transformed. The 2025 nodes are noted below. These muted energies will be working in the subconscious of everyone.

NORTH NODE

PISCES (NORTH)

From January 12 and for the rest of 2025 the North Node will be in the creative and compassionate sign of Pisces offering all humans the opportunity to be more loving and spiritual. It's a cosmic request to see with a spiritual eye, listen with a spiritual ear, and lead with a spiritual heart. Pisceans are dreamers and visionaries. We are asked to use our mind's eye to build heaven on earth. Be boundless in your belief and unlimited in your vision for yourself and what you desire. Avoid the Piscean trap of martyrdom and do your best to take steps to activate the new world, don't avoid doing the work (Virgo) it's your karmic destiny.

SOUTH NODE

VIRGO (SOUTH)

The opposite of karmic destiny may be thought of as our karmic history and it lies in the zodiac on the opposite side of the axis of Pisces, which is Virgo. Our South Node sign shows what hurdles we need to clear or habits we can ditch. It's entirely possible that we've lived in a world hell-bent on work, work, work and a high level of productivity when what would serve us more is to slow down and dream (Pisces). Virgo has a heart of gold but has a bad habit of nit-picking to the point of expecting perfection. It's time to stop judging and allow everyone to just be their imperfect selves.

Enjoy the Pisces-Virgo North and South node stories as they play out for the next 18 months.

✷ https://choosebigchange.com ✷

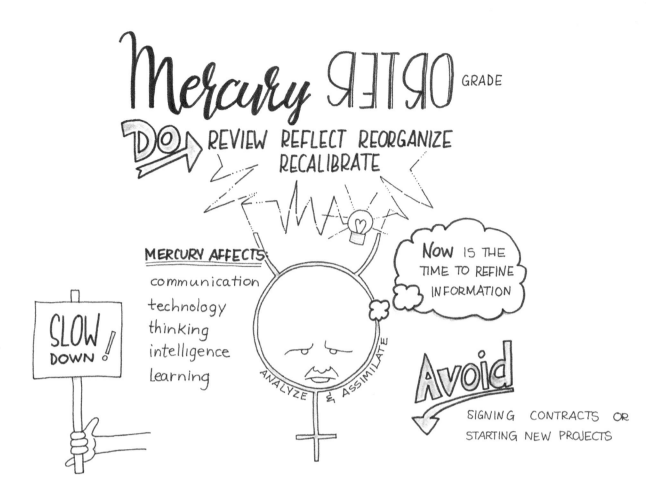

The key to using a retrograde well is to use the time to assimilate information from lessons learned in recent weeks. The theme for each of the Mercury Retrogrades is below along with questions you can use for reflection.

MARCH 15 – APRIL 7 IN ARIES | REVISITING LEADERSHIP

- What am I still afraid to be or do?
- How can being bold serve me and humanity?
- What generative energy can I be to be individually me?

JULY 18 – AUGUST 11 IN LEO | REIGNITING PASSION

- What space can I be to receive more inspiration?
- What is the benefit of being more expressive?
- Where has my passion fizzled, and why?

NOV 9 – 29 IN SAGITTARIUS | REINSPECTING ROUTINES

- What space can I be for new ways of thinking to find me?
- What is the benefit of going in a new direction?
- How can being open-minded serve me?

♡ Love the Energy Almanac? Tag us on social media: @TheEnergyAlmanac ♡

Page 17

Numerology

◇◆◇

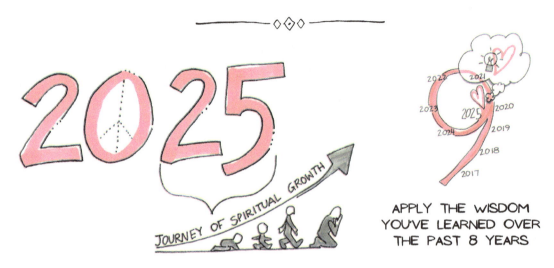

JOURNEY OF SPIRITUAL GROWTH

APPLY THE WISDOM
YOU'VE LEARNED OVER
THE PAST 8 YEARS

Everything in the universe is energy, including numbers. Energetic vibrations of numbers carry out into the universal field. Each number can be decoded and interpreted to add meaning to addresses, birthdates, times, and even phone numbers. This ancient art has been around for thousands of years; we bring this ancient art into the Energy Almanac and weave the meaning of numbers with the astrological energetic readings. This year's numerology is included in each of the monthly overview sections.

The year ahead, 2025, in general has its own unique fingerprint. Let's break it down.

21st century = The number 21 is about truth telling

2000 = Two's are feminine energy and represent peace and harmony. With the zero typifying the light of consciousness, imagine Source energy illuminating the path toward balance.

2 + 5 = 7 The 25th year of this century adds up to the number 7, the number of silence, spirit, and nature. This secondary story in the 2025 year will underpin everything else.

2 + 0 + 2 + 5 = 9 2025 is a 9 numerological year and here we have the closing of a cycle and the wisdom that comes with having been through all of it. It's a time to review the information you've gathered over the previous 8 years and prepare yourself for the decade ahead.

Numerology articles written by Tam Veilleux, artist, alchemist, astrology-junkie
www.choosebigchange.com | IG @TheEnergyAlmanac

✳ https://choosebigchange.com ✳

Out of the Shadow

— ◊◆◊ —

Every degree of the Zodiac and every Gate in Human Design presents us with a spectrum of energies ranging from high to low. It is up to each of us to choose at what level we are going to act. For example, Taurus energy can be very good at building something—a garden, a relationship, or financial well-being. However, in its lowest expression, Taurus can be fearful of living in poverty, get stuck in rigid patterns, and build upon weak foundations. Life presents us with opportunities, and we choose how we are going to show up.

Each week of the Energy Almanac, you are presented with possible shadow energies. The purpose is not for you to be in fear or judgment of yourself or others, but rather to gain perspective on the choices you get to make. How you respond to life's challenges and opportunities is where your free will lies. Becoming aware of the possible pitfalls helps you choose more carefully.

In part, the shadow energies come from my experience with The Gene Keys by Richard Rudd. The Gene Keys presents energy as a hologram where we can choose to be at the shadow, gift, or siddhi level—siddhi is a Sanskrit word meaning "the highest level." Much of the time, we unconsciously live in the shadow field where our fears drive our behavior. I hope that by bringing the potential shadows up to conscious awareness, we can become more deliberate in reaching higher vibrational frequencies.

How do we work with shadow energy? The first step is to read through the potential expression of the shadow energy for the week. Then step back and become the observer in your life. Is this shadow energy one you are familiar with? Do you struggle to release yourself from fear? Are there people or situations in your life that trigger a fear response? By stepping back, you can observe the answers to these questions from a neutral point of view. The next step is to prepare your response to these triggers should they arise. For example, if you face the fear of inadequacy, create a mini-dialogue to empower yourself. The opposite of inadequacy is wisdom. You could say to yourself, "I hold a depth of wisdom I can use in this situation."

Remember, you are in the driver's seat, and get to choose how you will move through fear and shadow energy!

JANET HICKOX, Gemini, is a gifted teacher, intuitive astrologer, and visionary who uses Astrology, Human Design, and the Gene Keys to help people live their authentic lives. Through a Human Design Astrology consult, she helps you unlock the key ingredients that make you unique, opening doors to freedom and success! A session with Janet gives you the valuable insight you need to make brilliant decisions in all areas of your life, including relationships, health, finances, and career. Janet believes, "To know oneself is priceless and leads to being in the right place, at the right time, with the right opportunities to thrive!"

www.living-astrology.com | IG @livingastrologywithjanet | FB @LivingAstrology

From Our Contributors

GEMSTONES

Gemstones each carry their own special kind of magic. Their location of origin and their physical make-up combine to emit a vibrational energy that can be felt by the carrier of the individual stone. Indigenous groups have been using gemstones in healing ceremonies for thousands of years. Whether you are warding off negative energies or amplifying the better ones, gemstones will work with you to bring lasting results. This year's gemstones were carefully selected to match the astrology of each month.

WAYS TO USE GEMSTONES:

- Wear stone(s) daily to immerse yourself in the energies. Keep one in your pocket or wear a bracelet or piece of jewelry with the suggested stones.
- Use for meditation and breathwork. Hold the stone in your hand or let it rest on the chakras it corresponds to.
- Use a set of gemstone meditation beads with the suggested mantras for each month. Speak your goals and targets aloud while holding a stone.
- Use stones to aid your sleep. Keep stones under your pillow, on your bedside table, or hanging over your bed.
- Keep stones where you spend a good portion of your day: at your office, on your desk, the living room, the kitchen, your car, or your bedroom.

The 2025 gemstones section was guided by Autumn Banks (Capricorn), energy worker and intuitive. Follow her journey online.

FB @autumn.banks | IG @autumnbanks86

ESSENTIAL OILS

◇ ◆ ◇

Using essential oils is an easy way to tap into the energy of each month. The use of essential oils is recorded in ancient times. Oils of plants were used for religious rituals and as medicine, too. Science and research have made the use of essential oils in contemporary time a smart addition to other traditional therapies.

Oils carry energies unique to each variety. They have a vibration. Over time, as you use them you will start to know exactly which oil will serve you best and at what time.

When choosing essential oils, it is vital to make sure you are using completely pure oil that is certified as pure tested grade oils (CPTG) and is ethically sourced. Don't be afraid to pair your oil with your current life circumstance according to your intuitive nudges as 2025 does suggest a strong use of your inner knowings. Let our essential oil articles for the year be a starting point for your journey with this plant-based therapy.

Check online resources or with a certified aromatherapist for further information about how best to use your essential oils. Some require a carrier oil in order to use them. Check safety guidelines often.

STEPHANIE VEILLEUX, Aquarius, is a Certified Aromatherapist for 18 years and a Childbirth Doula. A passionate lover of nature, Stephanie has been studying and using essential oils for holistic healing to help bring balance and peace to people's lives—particularly to children, women and their growing families. Her business is Lavendoula. When she's not working with women and children easing the burdens of everyday life, you can find her proudly mothering her two children, smothering herself in warm sunlight, dancing sassy burlesque or viewing the world behind a camera.

IG @lavendoulaME

Scan here

BONUS TOOLS & RESOURCES TO SUPPORT YOUR JOURNEY
WWW.CHOOSEBIGCHANGE.COM/PAGES/BONUS25

♡ Love the Energy Almanac? Tag us on social media: @TheEnergyAlmanac ♡

Page 21

RHYTHMS, ROUTINES & RITUALS

Ever notice how our vibes sync up with the universe's playlist? It's like having a secret handshake with energy, planets, seasons, and the whole shebang. Tapping into these cosmic beats with simple rituals? That's the game-changer.

Keeping an eye on the astrological energy and seasons is like learning the dance moves of the universe. Letting go, embracing fresh starts, and finding beauty in every phase—it's a whole cosmic ballet. Syncing up with these cycles plugs us into the world and makes us feel like part of the universe's big, awesome orchestra.

Rituals and routines are like life anchors in this wild dance. A morning meditation, throwing love at the universe in a gratitude ritual (my personal jam), or just strolling in nature (you'll find that to be especially helpful in September)—these intentional moves keep us grounded. They're our daily dose of zen, a chance to hit pause and soak in the good energy.

Honoring the rhythm of energy, seasons, and life with these rituals isn't just a lifestyle choice; it's a life philosophy. Embracing these cosmic cycles isn't just unlocking a door—it's flinging it wide open to a life that's balanced, mindful, and purposeful. Let's groove to the rhythm of this wild ride we call life.

KRISTEN RZASA, is a Pisces and a Manifesting Generator who is passionate about cultivating authentic conversation among women. As a holistic business and life strategist, she helps people find a brand-new rhythm in their bodies, days, businesses, and lives. She combines her corporate leadership experience with her background in health and wellness to guide clients to elevate their mindset, enhance their energy, expand their time, and enrich their environment. As a result, clients become strategic, focused, and energetically aligned so that they can crush their goals without crushing their souls. She is a speaker, productivity expert, intenSati leader and wellness educator.

www.KristenRzasa.com | IG @kristenhrzasa | FB @kristen.rzasa

✶ https://choosebigchange.com ✶

WISDOM DIARIES

◇ ◇ ◇

Dear Reader,

Welcome to "The Wisdom Diaries," a collection of heartfelt letters addressed to your ancestors, seeking their timeless knowledge and guidance as you navigate the journey of life in the year to come. In these pages, you'll embark on a sacred journey of exploration, delving into the depths of your familial lineage and reclaiming the wisdom that has been passed down through generations. Each letter is a testament to the power of connection across time and space, as you reach out to the ancestors with an open heart and open mind, inviting them to share their insights, their stories, and their love. Through these letters, honor is bestowed to the legacy of those who came before, recognizing the profound impact they have had on shaping who you are today.

"The Wisdom Diaries" is more than just a compilation of letters; it is a testament to the power of healing and forgiveness. Delving into the ancestral past, and confronting the wounds and traumas that have been passed down from generation to generation will allow you to recognize the ways that the pain of your ancestors might still reverberate within you today.

In acknowledging these wounds, you will also find an opportunity for healing and transformation. Through the act of sending forgiveness through time and space, you'll have the opportunity to release yourself from the burden of carrying ancestral pain and embrace a path of healing and reconciliation. By recognizing that the ancestors were human beings, flawed and imperfect, doing the best they could with the knowledge and resources available to them at the time we allow them to heal their trauma and pain on the other side of the veil.

In claiming your generational strengths and reclaiming your ancestral wisdom, you not only honor the resilience and perseverance of those who came before, but also pave the way for a brighter and more harmonious future. "The Wisdom Diaries" is a testament to the power of love, compassion, and forgiveness, as you strive to heal the wounds of the past and create a legacy of wisdom and grace for generations to come.

I invite you to join in on this journey of exploration and discovery, as you seek the guidance of our ancestors and embrace the transformative power of forgiveness and healing. May "The Wisdom Diaries" inspire you to reclaim your own ancestral wisdom and to step into the fullness of your own divine potential.

With love and gratitude,
Jane Redlon

JANE REDLON, Capricorn, channels profound healing through her extensive experience in Usui Reiki, complemented by a range of quantum energy healing modalities. Passionately driven by her life purpose, she mirrors the Divine essence within every soul she encounters. Jane's journey has been marked by confronting trauma, self-love struggles, and embracing vulnerability, fostering an environment where others can safely unveil their truths. Guided by her belief in the interconnectedness of all life, she champions unity, inviting others to embrace their authenticity and join in the harmonious tapestry of life's interconnected threads.

FB @janesays85 | IG @jredlon85

Energy Almanac 2025 Edition

MONTHLY ORACLE PLAY

Ask a good question and get a good answer. That's the goal of the Energy Almanac's new Monthly Oracle Play section. Here you are encouraged to use your favorite oracle deck to give yourself messages and hints about the month ahead.

How to use this section:

- Pick a deck you truly enjoy working with or one that you want to understand more deeply.
- At the first of each month settle in to a quiet spot with your journal, Energy Almanac, pen, and deck.
- Light a candle and set an intention to receive information from your Higher Self for the highest and best good of your spiritual journey.
- Shuffle the deck as you take several deep breaths and ask the question:

"What do I need to know about the month ahead?"

- When you are ready, cut the deck and stack one pile on top of the other.
- Spread the deck out in front of you and then let your hand and intuition guide you to pick cards one at a time. Pick three to five cards.
- With each card you pick, lay them out in the spread we've drawn for you in the Monthly Oracle Play sections of this book.
- Use your intuition to define what you see in the cards in front of you. Look for symbols and interpret them. Feel the meanings of the cards through color, mood, expressions.
- Use the space provided each month to write down the cards and notes about what you are sensing.

Set a reminder for the last day of the month to review your oracle reading. Make notes about how the month played out and how accurate your reading was. **Be sure to write to us and let us know how it went. Tag us on Instagram using #EnergyAlmanac or @TheEnergyAlmanac.**

CARD 1
CARD 2
CARD 3
CARD 4
CARD 5

https://choosebigchange.com

READER BONUSES

❖◆❖

You like gifts, don't you?

We have curated a fun collection of low-cost items, discounts, special codes, and free things from excellent small companies that we think you'd like to know about.

FREE MINI MOON JOURNALS

DISCOUNTS ON ORACLE READINGS

QUARTERLY RHYTHM ROUTINES

DISCOUNT CODES
AUDIO DOWNLOADS
FUN STUFF
HELPFUL IDEAS

SCAN HERE

Visit this link often to see what we've added:
CHOOSEBIGCHANGE.COM/PAGES/BONUS25

♡ Love the Energy Almanac? Tag us on social media: @TheEnergyAlmanac ♡

Energy Almanac 2025 Edition

Page 25

2025

January

M	T	W	T	F	S	S
		1	2	3	4	5
6	7	8	9	10	11	12
13	14	15	16	17	18	19
20	21	22	23	24	25	26
27	28	29	30	31		

February

M	T	W	T	F	S	S
					1	2
3	4	5	6	7	8	9
10	11	12	13	14	15	16
17	18	19	20	21	22	23
24	25	26	27	28		

March

M	T	W	T	F	S	S
					1	2
3	4	5	6	7	8	9
10	11	12	13	14	15	16
17	18	19	20	21	22	23
24	25	26	27	28	29	30
31						

April

M	T	W	T	F	S	S
	1	2	3	4	5	6
7	8	9	10	11	12	13
14	15	16	17	18	19	20
21	22	23	24	25	26	27
28	29	30				

May

M	T	W	T	F	S	S
			1	2	3	4
5	6	7	8	9	10	11
12	13	14	15	16	17	18
19	20	21	22	23	24	25
26	27	28	29	30	31	

June

M	T	W	T	F	S	S
						1
2	3	4	5	6	7	8
9	10	11	12	13	14	15
16	17	18	19	20	21	22
23	24	25	26	27	28	29
30						

July

M	T	W	T	F	S	S
	1	2	3	4	5	6
7	8	9	10	11	12	13
14	15	16	17	18	19	20
21	22	23	24	25	26	27
28	29	30	31			

August

M	T	W	T	F	S	S
				1	2	3
4	5	6	7	8	9	10
11	12	13	14	15	16	17
18	19	20	21	22	23	24
25	26	27	28	29	30	31

September

M	T	W	T	F	S	S
1	2	3	4	5	6	7
8	9	10	11	12	13	14
15	16	17	18	19	20	21
22	23	24	25	26	27	28
29	30					

October

M	T	W	T	F	S	S
	1	2	3	4	5	
6	7	8	9	10	11	12
13	14	15	16	17	18	19
20	21	22	23	24	25	26
27	28	29	30	31		

November

M	T	W	T	F	S	S
					1	2
3	4	5	6	7	8	9
10	11	12	13	14	15	16
17	18	19	20	21	22	23
24	25	26	27	28	29	30

December

M	T	W	T	F	S	S
1	2	3	4	5	6	7
8	9	10	11	12	13	14
15	16	17	18	19	20	21
22	23	24	25	26	27	28
29	30	31				

IMPORTANT DATES

Living-Astrology

with Janet Hickox

Human Design + Astrology Readings + Coaching

UNDERSTAND YOUR TRUE SELF & LIVE YOUR BEST LIFE!

FREE **Get Your Personalized Human Design Astrology Chart and Report**

Learn:

- how to make the best decisions for you
- how to have successful relationships
- how to use your energy in a healthy and sustainable way

GO TO: WWW.LIVING-ASTROLOGY.COM

FUN, FRESH FINE ART & FUN ART WITH

tamV

"Art is incredibly, crazily worth- while. And it's an invitation to the Divine."

-JORDAN PETERSON,
CONTEMPORARY THOUGHT LEADER

BUY ART TODAY! VISIT:

TAMVEILLEUX.COM
@BIGPINKSTUDIO

January

◇ ◆ ◇

Go with the Flow

DECEMBER 30–JANUARY 5

DO choose your battles wisely this week.
DO NOT cling to outdated fear patterns.

JANUARY 6–12

DO work on planning your goals.
DO NOT be apprehensive about the
collective future.

JANUARY 13–19

DO pay attention to dreamtime.
DO NOT let anxiety erode your peace.

JANUARY 20–26

DO be thinking about the year ahead.
DO NOT jump at opportunities just yet.

JANUARY 27–FEBRUARY 2

DO offer heart-to-heart connections.
DO NOT avoid a month-end review.

HOW CAN I EMPLOY EMPATHY, CREATIVITY, AND COMPASSION MORE FULLY?

JANUARY 13, 5:27 PM

FULL MOON AT 24° CANCER
ILLUMINATING INNER KNOWLEDGE

JANUARY 29, 7:36 AM

NEW MOON AT 9° AQUARIUS
SHOCKING IDEAS OF THE FUTURE

Energy Almanac 2025 Edition

Month At-A-Glance

Write in the dates of this month before taking a few minutes to make notes of specific astrological time periods as they intersect with your own life happenings. You may even choose to highlight those time periods in green and red to remind yourself of easy and difficult days.

MONDAY	TUESDAY	WEDNESDAY	THURSDAY	FRIDAY	SATURDAY	SUNDAY

 Notes

January

◇ ◇ ◇

The cooler weather and dark nights of winter are engulfing us now and yet, we must mush forward, one foot at a time into the new year. Welcome to January 2025 where we begin with three planets retrograde. Mars, Jupiter, and Uranus are all giving us pause. Mars' position in Cancer has us practicing the control of our emotions and co-cooning as often as possible; it's not such a bad thing for January. Jupiter in Gemini has us questioning the world and its education systems while Uranus in Taurus is still asking us to review the economy and make corrections as needed. It's a slow time period, for sure. With two personal planets in water signs, emotions are high and the love is big. On the 11th, when humanity's lunar North Node changes to Pisces, the world may finally "go with the flow." We will be subconsciously urged toward empathy, creativity, and compassion, an influence with us for the next 18 months. January will end with Aquarian activity in the form of a New Moon, the Sun, and Mercury all in this futuristic, friendly, and humanitarian sign, perhaps pulling us all in a direction that serves the greater good. Only time will tell how this plays out over the next twelve months.

TRANSITS

1/2	**Venus enters Pisces**
1/6	**Mars Retrograde enters Cancer**
1/8	**Mercury enters Capricorn**
1/11	**North Node enters Pisces**
1/13	**Full Moon at 24° Cancer,** read moon article
1/19	**Sun enters Aquarius, Happy birthday, Aquarians!**
1/24	**National Peanut Butter Day**
1/27	**Mercury enters Aquarius**
1/29	**New Moon at 9° Aquarius,** read moon article
1/30	**Uranus direct in Taurus**

RESOURCES

Numerology: 10 month in a 9 year

Gemstones: Ocean Jasper, Herkimer Diamond

Oils: Chamomile, Orange

Rituals: Mindfulness Meditation, Carve Out Some White Space, Embrace Imperfection

Wisdom Diaries: Discernment

ORACLE PLAY

"What do I need to know about the month ahead?"

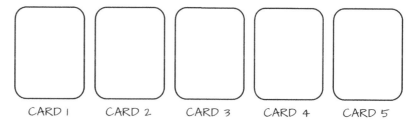

CARD 1   CARD 2   CARD 3   CARD 4   CARD 5

_____

_____

_____

_____

JANUARY PREDICTIONS

MONDAY, DECEMBER 30 – SUNDAY, JANUARY 5 | **MOONS:** CAPRICORN, AQUARIUS, PISCES

The new year is here and our journey begins with a serious attitude and the desire to bring order or set a foundation under goals as the moon in Capricorn shines down on humanity Monday through Wednesday. It is perfect for creating a plan for the month, quarter or year. How fortunate that on Friday Venus, the planet of relations, slides into the creative and empathetic sign of Pisces where she will amplify our visions, creativity, and compassion for the next few weeks. Be sure to purchase a new sketchbook or journal for making a visual representation of your dreams. Vision board anyone?? With grandmother moon sliding into Pisces over the weekend, it seems the perfect time to pull out your scissors, magazines, and glue and get busy.

GIFT & SHADOW THIS WEEK: *With the Sun in Gate 38-Struggle, choose your battles wisely this week. That means if something is worth fighting for, it is appropriate to continue, and if it is not worth it, then time to free yourself from the struggle. As we near the end of the nodal transit through Aries/Libra, it's time to resolve the issues we have around living our lives authentically. Stop the people-pleasing, and please yourself. Others will be happy if you're happy and if they're not...that's their issue!*

MONDAY, JANUARY 6 – SUNDAY, JANUARY 12 | **MOONS:** ARIES, TAURUS, GEMINI

Have you noticed how fiercely emotional you've been over the past few months? You've been feeling protective and truly enjoying home life over the last many weeks. With Mars, the planet of action, in the emotional and intuitive sign of Cancer moving retrograde Monday until late February, all of this could shift. A slow down such as this could find you internalizing your emotions rather than feeling them as you had been. Be mindful of this trait because stuffed emotion can be dangerous to your health. Cocooning in order to feel the feels is a safe way to handle what needs to come up. If you're triggered early in the week on Wednesday Mercury, planetary analyzer, moves into Capricorn and you'll have the resources to make a plan for both your goals and your emotional well being.

A key aspect for 2025 occurs on Friday when the North Node enters Pisces and the entire collective is led toward more compassion, boundless visions, and a large dose of soulfulness. This important lunar node shift can be read about on page 16.

GIFT & SHADOW THIS WEEK: *The current shadow energy centers on the theme of survival, particularly our apprehension about not making it through. Fortunately, there exists a straightforward solution to navigate this energy—redirecting our attention towards the light. We find ourselves in a phase where we can shed the deeply rooted tribal fears by embracing an initiation into a novel collective existence on this planet. Is it challenging? Not really, unless we tenaciously cling to outdated fear patterns, preventing ourselves from experiencing true freedom.*

MONDAY, JANUARY 13 – SUNDAY, JANUARY 19

MOONS: CANCER, LEO, VIRGO

A week to work with the moons is what lies ahead, Little Pretzel. It begins with a beautiful Full Moon in Cancer on Monday. Nurture your soul, listen to your intuition and do some healing work as you clear out what might be in the way of last month's goals. Read more about it in this month's Moon articles. The rest of the week is easy-peasy as the moons carry you through self-expression and perhaps feeling frisky before ending the week with a sense of practicality and perhaps a little volunteerism in the name of service to humanity. Sunday brings Aquarian season as the sun steps into the zodiac represented by the astronaut's space suit and you begin to notice thoughts about the future, some of which might involve the betterment of the group. If you take us up on our advice, snap a picture and tag us on social media. We love cheering on our readers. Use @TheEnergyAlmanac

GIFT & SHADOW THIS WEEK: *If you discover yourself entangled in fear and worry, you've likely surrendered to the prevailing shadow energy. It's probable that you've been overly entrenched in your thoughts rather than residing in your heart, where anxiety can subtly erode your sense of sanctity. Ats the peak of this energy, we find harmony in discerning what is necessary and placing trust in the belief that everything unfolds precisely as it should. While it's essential to be mindful of the details, avoid letting them overpower your sense of balance.*

MONDAY, JANUARY 20 – SUNDAY, JANUARY 26

MOONS: LIBRA, SCORPIO, SAGITTARIUS

Ahhh, another relatively quiet week is here for you to enjoy. The lunations of the moon in Libra, Scorpio, and Sagittarius offer you the opportunity for growth. Challenge yourself to research these three zodiac signs and then notice what you can about how you react and respond as the moon moves through these constellations this week. For fun on Friday whip out your favorite jar of peanut butter and bake or smear something yummy and share it with a friend or partner. It's National Peanut Butter Day! (Tag us in your social post, too!) Sunday could provide some stimulating thoughts as Saturn in Pisces triggers Pluto in Aquarius. Your visions of a seriously soul-fueled future might be worth jotting down.

GIFT & SHADOW THIS WEEK: *Happy Human Design New Year (on January 22)! While we celebrate a new year in the Human Design System, it is still a time for connecting to the dreamtime. Dreamtime is the pause between being and doing. Take time to look ahead at what you want to do this year, but don't take steps yet. Consider where you might need to make some changes and how you might want to grow and evolve into the year. In the shadow this week, we may "jump" at opportunities and find ourselves having to reel back in from being overly impulsive.*

Scan here

BOOK BONUSES INCLUDE DISCOUNT CODES, EBOOKS, SPECIAL REPORTS, AUDIO FILES AND SPECIAL OFFERS. TO GET ALL THE GOODIES, GO TO WWW.CHOOSEBIGCHANGE.COM/PAGES/BONUS25

♡ Fun, fresh, transformational products + services: https://choosebigchange.com ♡

MONDAY, JANUARY 27 – SUNDAY, FEBRUARY 2

MOONS: CAPRICORN, AQUARIUS, PISCES

It wasn't enough that the Sun, and Pluto are in forward-thinking Aquarius; here comes Mercury to join the party. With Mercury in this position through mid-February notice technology and all that comes with it. Aquarius rules invisible waves and the higher mind. Mercury is the lower mind. Together they collaborate for a holistic view of the future and the many potentials available if we work together. It's important work worth thinking about. Notice your intuition is amplified and your logical brain can use the information in imaginative ways. Friday brings the New Moon also in the sign of Aquarius and here we have more of the same. It's the perfect moon to gather in a group and share insights with friends. Sound healing, which works with frequency, could be highlighted. January ends over the weekend and it's a perfect time to review the month. What did you notice? How did you feel? Is there anything you're particularly proud of? A good review pays off in spades. Saturday is February 1 and it's time to set new goals.

GIFT & SHADOW THIS WEEK: *We all want to feel like we belong in a family, tribe, or community. This week's shadow of the Sun in Gate 19-Sensitivity, concerns when that turns into neediness, clinginess, or codependency. Increasing our heart-to-heart connections with others begins with a healthy sense of self-worth, self-love, and value. We might also need to watch out for re-telling old stories of abandonment, "nobody wants me," or other negative narratives. You belong, you are worthy, and you are valued!*

FUN, FRESH, TRANSFORMATIONAL COMPANION PRODUCTS TO HELP MAKE 2025 AMAZING ARE AVAILABLE AT:

WWW.CHOOSEBIGCHANGE.COM

January Moon Work

JANUARY 13, 5:27 PM	ILLUMINATING INNER
FULL MOON AT 24° CANCER	KNOWLEDGE

The first full lunar illumination strikes a chord at home and drives emotions high. While wanting to stay home and be cozy in your bathrobe, notice your serious demeanor and strong capacity for setting a foundation. The thoughts may be flavored by explorations of your own value system. With the moon playing nicely with Uranus you may receive great insights worth looking at that will bolster your future self.

Your imagination and intuition could be quite strong under this moon. There is an influence of Mars in Neptune trine Neptune in Pisces making internal knowledge strong. Beyond that, the atmosphere is perfect for gathering friends for a social and creative good time. The battle will be between cocooning (Cancer) and socializing (Venus and Jupiter in Gemini).

AFFIRMATION: *"I trust the knowledge that comes from within."*

MOON WORK:

- Meditate (Cancer and Pisces). Set your timer for 7 minutes asking the question "What do I need to know right now?" Capture it in your journal and trust what comes through.
- Plan a creative event with friends (Venus and Jupiter in Gemini). A paint and sip evening or karaoke could be perfect. Better yet, learn how to work with singing bowls for deep healing.
- Bolster your self-worth (Uranus in Taurus). List all of your skills and talents, then ask your family members (Cancer) to name your skills and talents. Add their thoughts to yours.

_____

_____

_____

_____

_____

_____

_____

_____

_____

_____

_____

JANUARY 29, 7:36 AM
NEW MOON AT 9° AQUARIUS

 SHOCKING IDEAS OF THE FUTURE

In the crisp cold of January enters the Aquarius New Moon where the dreams of the future are formed in the dark. There is plenty in play and your expectations may both surprise and delight you as your lower mind receives information worth ruminating on as it relates to the transformation landscape of humanitarianism, digital experiments, and socializing. Be sure to capture those potentially shocking ideas and how you might participate in much-needed changes.

There is a harmonious trine between the Sun, Moon, and Jupiter that could instigate your sociability or generate questions. The topic of conversations could range from the use of AI to how we educate ourselves.

The conversations certainly could be deep and spiritual. Your inner eye may see exactly what needs to happen next if you partner with Saturn and apply discipline to your spiritual practice today. Don't be surprised if you feel "in the flow" as Mars is in Cancer and Venus is in Pisces and they are playing in the cosmos with Uranus. The three could find you with a full heart and loads of self-compassion proving to you that you truly do deserve all that is coming to you.

AFFIRMATION: *"All of life flows to me easily now and in the future."*

MOON WORK:

- Aquarians are futuristic, have a heart storm! Make a 100 wishes list as you tap into your desires for the months ahead.
- Work in a non-linear fashion using intuitive writing. Have paper out, put the pen in your hand and just doodle circles as you ask "What matters now?" Let the answers roll out of you without thinking about them.
- This cold night requires hot chocolate and friends. Have everyone bring their favorite mug to your outdoor fire pit. Warm the milk and chocolate of choice, fill your favorite mugs, top with whipped cream then sprinkle with cinnamon and a dash of cayenne for something to warm you inside and out.

_____

_____

_____

_____

_____

_____

_____

_____

_____

_____

_____

Numerology

Numerologically this is a ten month in a nine year.
January = 1 and 2025 = 9; 1 + 9 = 10

One, or ten is the beginning of a new cycle. This is perfect for the first month of a year that challenges you to bring wisdom into all you do. The one of the ten is new beginnings and initiation, and the zero is God's light shining on you. You are reminded that you are starting a new journey in January.

Gemstones & Oils

GEMSTONES

Ocean Jasper Helps you go with the flow; adds patience, fluidity, joy, nurturing, and compassion.

Herkimer Diamond This stone brings visions, attunement, aids in dream recall, enhances meditation, purifies energy, and connects the heart and Spirit together.

OILS

Chamomile *Chamaemelum nobile*
Acceptance, calm control, emotional balancing, heart warming
Blends well w/ citrus oils, Frankincense & Geranium

Chamomile has beautiful emotional regulating qualities, the calming nature of this oil allows the heart and mind to align bringing about a sense of ease, going with the flow nature. It works with the throat chakra and encourages calm self expression all while staying grounded. Chamomile says let go of all that holds you back.

Orange *Citrus sinensis*
Ease, adaptability, optimism, abundance
Blends well w/ Peppermint, Citrus, Cedarwood and Chamomiles

Her youthful glow and bright uplifting personality is constantly encouraging an optimistic perspective on the future with curiosity, feeling light and easy. These are the qualities of orange. She reminds us to stay open minded, opportunities are coming.

Chamomile and Orange blended together help aid the "digestion of life."

_____

_____

_____

♡ Fun, fresh, transformational products + services: https://choosebigchange.com ♡

Rhythms, Routines & Rituals

Let's go with the flow to live more authentically, enjoy the present moment, and navigate the twists and turns of January with greater ease and grace.

Try these experiments on for size this month:

- **Mindfulness Meditation:** Practicing mindfulness meditation, even for two minutes, can ground you in the present. It allows you to accept things as they are and flow with the present moment without resistance. I like to do this before getting out of bed. Sit quietly and simply focus on your breath. Try inhaling for five counts, holding for five, and exhaling for five. Rinse and repeat.

- **Carve Out Some White Space:** Schedules these days are jam packed. Let's leave some open space in that calendar. Instead of rigidly adhering to a fixed plan, stay flexible and be open to what comes your way. I use a sticker or washi tape in my ol' school planner to leave open time in my schedule.

- **Embrace Imperfection:** Perfection is overrated. Accepting that things won't always go as planned and being okay with imperfections can alleviate stress and anxiety. Embrace the journey rather than focusing solely on the outcome. Try taking imperfect action on a goal or task.

These practices will enhance your ability to navigate January's ups and downs with more ease and resilience. And when life throws a curveball, or something pops up to derail you, just yell "plot twist!," and keep going. Learn more about getting into flow, grab my bonus material.

_____

_____

_____

_____

_____

_____

_____

_____

_____

ENERGY ALMANAC CALL TO ACTION: Did you have an a-ha moment this month? If so, be brave! Employ your courage and share your insights on social media. Tag @TheEnergyAlmanac so we can cheer you on!

✷ Get your book bonus offers: www.choosebigchange.com/pages/bonus25 ✷

Wisdom Diaries

Dear Grandma,

Life has been throwing its usual curveballs my way lately, and I'm finding myself losing clarity. I find that I'm getting confused easily and twisted up about the right course of action on so many levels. You always taught me the importance of discernment, and only embracing something once it resonates deep within. I'm reaching out for your guidance on navigating these murky waters, because I know you have the life experience to help me in this way.

Your wisdom has been a guiding light for our family, and I know your perspective on spiritual discernment could provide me with invaluable clarity. How do you tell the difference between genuine spiritual guidance and the noise of ego or societal expectations? And how can I strengthen my connection to my inner truth and purpose? It is important for me to feel safe in my faith, and sometimes there are too many voices with too many opinions.

I'm eager to hear about your experiences and insights.

> With deep gratitude and love,
> Your Grandchild

My Sweet Grandchild,

Your letter fills my heart with joy, and I'm touched by your yearning for wisdom. Navigating the realm of the Spirit is a journey of the heart—one that requires patience, self-reflection, and a willingness to be vulnerable with yourself.

In my own life, I've learned that clarity comes when you get real cozy with yourself and begin to connect with the divine spark that is inside us all. Pay attention to your gut feelings as they often carry the whispers of Spirit guiding your way. When you're uncertain, place your hand on your heart, take a few deep breaths, and ask the Creator to reveal the truth. Jot down what comes to you, and reflect on that inner wisdom often.

Don't let the noise of the world or the expectations of others sway you. Trust your heart's knowing and the Creator's guidance. Find moments of peace and quiet, where you can tune into your soul's gentle rhythm.

Remember, clarity isn't about having all the answers at once; it's about embracing the journey with curiosity, humility, and grace. Be patient with yourself and trust that you're exactly where you need to be.

And never forget, my dear, you're not alone on this journey. The love and light of the Divine are always with you, ready to support and guide you whenever you ask.

> With all my love,
> Your Grandma

♡ Fun, fresh, transformational products + services: https://choosebigchange.com ♡

Month End Review

◇ ◇ ◇

What was new, good, and different about this month?

_____
_____
_____
_____
_____
_____
_____
_____
_____
_____
_____
_____
_____
_____
_____
_____
_____
_____
_____
_____
_____
_____
_____

February

LESSONS OF THE HEART

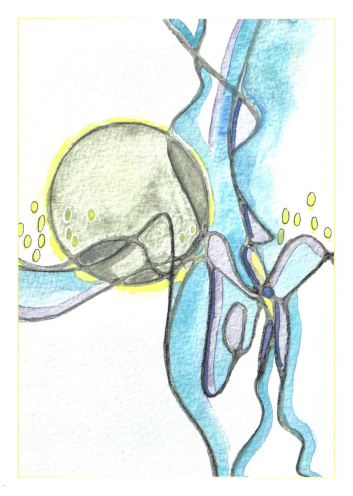

FEBRUARY 3-9

DO spend time dreaming into the future.
DO NOT be emotionally reactive.

FEBRUARY 10-16

DO be wary of adventuring to avoid
inner work.
DO NOT over-dissect your dreams.

FEBRUARY 17-23

DO empower others through compassion.
DO NOT think like a victim.

FEBRUARY 24-MARCH 2

DO be sure you're keeping your word.
DO NOT avoid a month-end review.

WHAT CAN I CHOOSE THAT FEELS GENERATIVE AND CREATIVE?

FEBRUARY 12, 8:53 AM

FULL MOON AT 24° LEO
DARING TO DANCE AND BE SEEN

FEBRUARY 27, 7:45 PM

NEW MOON AT 9° PISCES
KNOWING THE UNKNOWN

Energy Almanac 2025 EDITION

Month At-A-Glance

Write in the dates of this month before taking a few minutes to make notes of specific astrological time periods as they intersect with your own life happenings. You may even choose to highlight those time periods in green and red to remind yourself of easy and difficult days.

MONDAY	TUESDAY	WEDNESDAY	THURSDAY	FRIDAY	SATURDAY	SUNDAY

 Notes

February

◇◇◇

The shortest month of the year seems to set the tone for the year. On February 7th Neptune, planet of imagination and compassion, conjuncts the North Node in Pisces and we all have the opportunity to use our imagination, creativity, and compassion as well as our intuition to create a more loving society. Mid-month brings with it chatter of love and a flow that may have carried over from the week before as Pisces energy is quite present and encourages strong emotion. As the month closes and you wrap your shoulders with the warmest of blankets in the northern hemisphere, note thoughts of heart-centered leadership and what it means to you. Don't get caught escaping into day-dreaming. Take serious actions you can boldly go forward with in the weeks or months ahead.

TRANSITS

2/4	**Venus enters Aries**
2/7	**Neptune conjunct North Node**
2/12	**Full Moon at 24° Leo,** read moon article
2/14	**Mercury enters Pisces**
2/18	**Sun enters Pisces, Happy birthday, Pisceans!**
2/19	**International Tug of War Day**
2/23	**Mars direct in Cancer**
2/27	**New Moon at 9° Pisces,** read moon article

RESOURCES

Numerology: 11 month in a 9 year

Gemstones: Amazonite, Rhodochrosite

Oils: Ylang Ylang, Bay Laurel

Rituals: Heart Chakra Ritual

Wisdom Diaries: Compassion & Empathy

ORACLE PLAY

"What do I need to know about the month ahead?"

| CARD 1 | CARD 2 | CARD 3 | CARD 4 | CARD 5 |

_____

_____

_____

_____

_____

♡ Fun, fresh, transformational products + services: https://choosebigchange.com ♡

FEBRUARY PREDICTIONS

MONDAY, FEBRUARY 3 – SUNDAY, FEBRUARY 9	**MOONS:** ARIES, TAURUS, GEMINI

This week opens with a shift in energy as Venus, planet of love and money, dons the football uniform that represents Aries. Expect your personal leadership style to be more impassioned. Direct and daring, you may notice these changes inside of relationships. It seems perfect as Valentine's day approaches. Don't forget to make dinner reservations for next week. (Wink, wink!) Friday Neptune in its final degrees conjuncts the humanities north node, also thought of as our collective destiny. This important meeting of cosmic forces will add a pleasantly compassionate edge to the next few days. Spend some time dreaming and co-visioning a future where faith and love are first. Pull together a group of friends and speak aloud potential manifestations. Team work makes the dream work. Home alone? Do this work by yourself in full faith your wishes are heard and adding energy to the group desires.

GIFT & SHADOW THIS WEEK: *The first two weeks of February, from a Human Design perspective this year, offer us the opportunity to uplevel our lives through learning to be more emotionally intelligent. We are moving away from reactionary energy toward responsiveness. With the Sun at Gate 49-Revolution, there could be many triggers to cause emotional reactivity. The key is to understand that emotions catalyze a transformation and are not meant for us to react to. Rather, pause before reacting, check in with yourself on what the potential reactivity is about, and then choose a path forward that represents the highest consciousness possible.*

MONDAY, FEBRUARY 10 – SUNDAY, FEBRUARY 16	**MOONS:** CANCER, LEO, VIRGO

The bulk of this week's astrology is in the Moon's movement through Cancer, Leo, and then Virgo. Midweek is an expressive Full Moon in Leo that is so close to Valentine's Day that romance and charisma is sure to be prevalent. As an act of creative expression make "hearts and crafts" your Full Moon ritual. Cut them out in all shapes and sizes, write love notes on them and leave them to be found by others. Read more about the Full Moon in Leo in this month's resources pages. When date night rolls around on Friday and Mercury slides into Pisces sharing your vision or over-analyzing it during your Valentine dinner is possible. The thinking mind of Mercury communicates and Pisces is the creative, compassionate visionary who wants to flow through life. Be mindful through the end of February not to be too critical of your own potential, instead use your dissection skills to determine what's right, what can be amplified, or how you can get closer to fulfilling your dream.

GIFT & SHADOW THIS WEEK: *Jupiter, in Human Design, shows us the path of evolution in our consciousness ass a society. This week as Jupiter moves into Gate 35-Experience we are seeking the new adventure to explore what we have yet to experience. The shadow of this energy however, keeps us on an endless search for the new and keeps us stretching out the boundaries of our experiences. In other words, we need to be aware of a tendency to get caught up in the adrenaline rush or the "high" of the adventure, without really integrating what we have learned. The adventure isn't all about the outer world, but is more related to how we fill ourselves from the inside.*

MONDAY, FEBRUARY 17 – SUNDAY, FEBRUARY 23

MOONS: LIBRA, SCORPIO, SAGITTARIUS

Ahhh, respite again, Little Pretzel. This week is astrologically light. With moons in Libra, Scorpio, and Sagittarius you can assume a sense of balance and peace-keeping (Libra), an amplified interest in your own transformation (Scorpio), and an urge for adventure and fun. It's another week to catch your breath and simply reflect on the meaning of these zodiac signs. Research them and make notes of your own interactions with the energies at play. Side note: happy birthday cosmic Pisceans. Your birthday season begins on Tuesday. For the rest of us, you may note a bigger-than-normal sense of compassion for others. This typical trait of those born during February 18-March 20 cannot be denied. Also close to home and a classic quality is the habit of daydreaming. If you capture something juicy in your dream state, let us know. If you're looking for something to do, Wednesday is International Tug of War Day. If you have an old tie or rope, find a friend and have a playful game. If you have nobody to play with, check in with your canine, they typically love to tug. Tag @TheEnergyAlmanac on social media.

GIFT & SHADOW THIS WEEK: *The gift of abundance is ours not because of what we do but because of who we are—Divine Beings. The gift energy of Gate 55-Abundance this week reminds us of this reality. Unfortunately, we have built a society around doing and getting paid for what we do, thus minimizing the blessings of our intrinsic value. We then become more like "human doings" rather than human beings. This week, there is also fear and worry that we are not "enough" or will fail to be enough or have enough. Choose freedom from victim thinking.*

MONDAY, FEBRUARY 24 – SUNDAY, MARCH 2

MOONS: CAPRICORN, AQUARIUS, PISCES

How does it get any better than this? It's another gentle week that you can use for assimilating information and astro-energies. The disciplined and serious moon in Capricorn opens the week and by mid-week your friendliness is amplified before Thursday's New Moon in Pisces on a nine day (2 + 7 = 0) at the cosmic ninth degree in a cosmic nine year (2 + 0 + 2 + 5=9). A lunation full of wisdom and spiritual creativity is at play and the closing of a cycle so that you can evolve into something superior. This is a moon where you can dream a big dream and let your warm, loving heart really feel into the greatness of your vision. Our moon article in this month's resources offers more insight into how to best tap into this energy. This one is a good one for the sketchbook you may have purchased in January. Paint, collage, draw, or even stitch the energy that moves you on Thursday, February 27. Use the 28th to do your month end review and hopefully you made some goals under the new moon, so your March prep is complete. Sunday Venus journeys retrograde in the sign of Aries which tempers passion for the next few weeks. It's a good time to look at autonomy inside of relationships.

GIFT & SHADOW THIS WEEK: *The Channel 37-40 is where the Sun and Earth are this week. It is called the Channel of the Bargain. We enter into all kinds of agreements (aka bargains) and contracts, and this week challenges us to rewrite any of them that do not align with our integrity. Broken deals can lead to broken hearts, but renegotiating can be an art form allowing us to be at peace. Make honest and aligned agreements with others, keep your word, and peace will result. The shadow of this week comes up when we do not keep our word or enter into contracts that are not win-win.*

♡ Fun, fresh, transformational products + services: https://choosebigchange.com ♡

February Moon Work

FEBRUARY 12, 8:53 AM FULL MOON AT 24° LEO	○	DARING TO DANCE AND BE SEEN

The bright full moon in the playful sign of Leo is an opportunity to enjoy a daring dance under luminescent beams. One thing is for sure, Leo isn't afraid to express themselves. Your thinking mind may want to interrupt your gambol and get you focused on the future and you may be stimulated to disrupt the norm and just have a good romp for the sake of one thing alone: you are worthy of having a good time. The tension is between listening to your intuition and listening to logic.

If intuitive hits haven't become the norm, we'd be surprised! Mars is activating your emotions and instincts and under this lunation is partnering with Saturn for even more visioning about the next best ways of thriving.

Passionate partnerships working together for the good of the group along with bold individuals could have you strengthening and expanding your vision for personal leadership goals. There are plenty of leadership wounds to work with tonight. Chiron represents the collective sacred wound currently in Aries and is triggered by Venus, the Sun, and Grandmother Moon herself. Opportunity is knocking, will you take the chance to develop your pioneering spirit?

AFFIRMATION: *"I am brave enough to be seen expressing myself fully."*

MOON WORK:

- Dance under the moon as if no one is watching. Bundle up if you're in the United States, put on some raucous music and cut a rug releasing any stick angst, sadness, or fear.
- Write out the next level version of your goals and dreams.
- Describe yourself as a leader. List your best qualities and what needs work, make yourself a promise to develop in the areas that need it.
- Bolster your self-worth (Uranus in Taurus). List all of your skills and talents, then ask your family members (Cancer) to name your skills and talents. Add their thoughts to yours.

_____

_____

_____

_____

_____

_____

_____

_____

_____

FEBRUARY 27, 7:45 PM
NEW MOON AT 9° PISCES

KNOWING THE UNKNOWN

The new moon in Pisces is loaded with emotional opportunity, have tissues at hand. There are six planetary placements affecting your heart, imagination, and flow and with so much mutable energy that you could find yourself a bit fickle in creating your desires. Consider yourself warned to not fall into martyrdom or escapism either, with no boundaries it could be easy to lapse.

This lunation has front and center the sun and moon trine Mars in Cancer which is likely to amplify your emotion and your intuition. Tune in carefully today. Go slow and pay attention to the unseen. The collective subconscious is amplified by Neptune and your magical and spiritual nature should be the one thing that is very clear. Spend time in your personal art whether it's singing, painting, writing, or dancing, your soulfulness should shine today. The tension lies with Jupiter tugging at you to educate yourself or socialize though you may more innately want to escape.

Though your higher mind is fully engaged, let's not ignore Mercury and your frontal lobe. He is partnering with Saturn and bringing a practicality to everything that you will learn instinctively. So as the imaginings pour through you, you'll have support in planning them out, too.

If your bleeding and compassionate heart isn't tired yet, understand that the collective sacred wound involving your autonomy and individuality is at hand. You may find yourself inventing new ways to be bold.

AFFIRMATION: *"I am creating a loving relationship with Source energy."*

MOON WORK:

- Allow miracle-thinking to be present (Pisces energy), expand your vision for yourself and the world by dreaming bigger.
- Pisces is the end of the lunar year. Spend some time reflecting on the past 12 months and make some notes about how you'd like to adjust in the future. (Mercury/Saturn)
- Art, art, art. Find ways to express yourself in soulful ways.

♡ Fun, fresh, transformational products + services: https://choosebigchange.com ♡

Numerology

Numerologically this is an eleven month in a nine year.
February = 2 and 2025 = 9; 2 + 9 = 11

Eleven is the master number representing initiation and starting new endeavors. You'll have double the energy and twice the intuitive information to support yourself. If you get those subtle nudges, pay attention and don't be afraid to begin!

Gemstones & Oils

GEMSTONES

Amazonite Encourage truthfulness, connects you with nature and others, gives empowerment, sincerity, integrity, and allows deeper breathing.

Rhodochrosite Helps one be more present, attracts love (for yourself and from others), heals old emotional wounds and traumatic past lives, heightens compassion and inner worthiness.

OILS

Ylang Ylang *Cananga odorata*
Euphoric, sensual, dreaming
Blends well w/ Bergamot, Rose, Vanilla and Cedarwood

Sultry Ylang Ylang has a way of working into one's heart. Toning, calming and cooling the heart muscle encourages love to flow through. This empowers the passion and creativity of your heart to boldly take its place. She works passionately in your dreams encouraging you to bring them forward.

Bay Laurel *Laurus nobilis*
Ease, adaptability, optimism, abundance
Blends well w/ Ylang Ylang, Orange, Cedarwood, Clary Sage and Pine

Laurel stimulates the mind in a positive fashion, helping you feel confident and seeing your own potential as limitless. Laurel helps you take your dreams into creative action. He is a messenger known for producing intuitive and prophetic-like messages, opening the mind to direct communication with higher self. Wonderful for artists of all types who rely on divine connection to inspire their work.

_____

_____

_____

_____

Rhythms, Routines & Rituals

Let the love flow! Play with a heart chakra ritual to harness the energy of February and open yourself to the transformative power of love and compassion within and around you.

- Begin by creating a sacred space for your ritual, using elements such as candles, crystals, flowers, and soothing music to enhance the ambiance. Infuse each item with your intention for healing and balance in the heart center.

- Cleanse your space using sage or palo santo, or diffusing an essential oil. I like Lemongrass or Frankincense for this.

- Set your intention to release any negative energies and invite in the pure essence of love and compassion. Light the candles and take a few deep breaths to center yourself.

- Speak aloud or silently repeat affirmations that resonate with the energy of the heart chakra, infusing them with heartfelt intention. This could be something like:
    - "I am worthy of love and compassion."
    - "I open myself to give and receive love freely."
    - "I accept myself, as I am, in the world, as it is."

- Focus your attention on your heart and breathe deeply into this space.

- Reflect on your relationships, emotions, and experiences, with an open and compassionate heart and allow yourself to soak in the love.

Chakra rituals and visualizations are a powerful way to recalibrate during the changing energies of the year. This ritual can be replicated for any chakra and as often as needed. For more ways to incorporate ritual, grab my bonus material.

_____
_____
_____
_____
_____
_____
_____
_____
_____
_____
_____

♡ Fun, fresh, transformational products + services: https://choosebigchange.com ♡

Wisdom Diaries

Hey Auntie,

I wanted to chat with you about something that's been weighing on me lately. You know I look up to you and trust your advice, so I figured you might have some wisdom to share.

I've been dealing with a tricky situation involving a close person in my life. I love them to bits, but our relationship has been a bit rocky because of their behavior. They seem to always push my buttons and make things difficult, and it's been tough to keep my cool.

I know family and close friendships are important, and I want to be there for them, but it's hard to balance setting boundaries and still being empathetic. How do you manage to stay compassionate even when people are testing your limits? And how do you take care of yourself while still staying connected to loved ones?

You've always been a role model for me when it comes to keeping a level head and showing kindness, so I was hoping you could give me some pointers on how to handle this situation with grace. Thanks for always being there for me. I really appreciate your support and can't wait to hear your thoughts.

Lots of love,
Your Niece/Nephew

Hey there Kid,

Wow, I gotta say, your honesty and maturity in reaching out for advice really impresses me. It means a lot that you trust me enough to ask for help, and I'll do my best to give you some insights that might help with your situation.

First off, it's important to remember...that everyone's got their own stuff going on, ya know? Your friend, like all of us, is a complex human being with their own struggles and insecurities. Keeping that in mind can help you see things from their perspective and maybe cut them some slack, even when they're being a pain.

Try to dig a little deeper and figure out what might be driving their behavior. Maybe they're dealing with stuff you don't even know about, and it's coming out in the way they interact with you. Understanding where they're coming from can help you respond with more empathy and compassion. Remember, everyone is doing their very best, even when it doesn't seem that way, or their best isn't good enough. Sometimes life hits us hard and things become heavy or difficult. Extending compassion to others, and to ourselves, in these situations is generally the kindest thing to do.

Setting boundaries is key too. It's totally okay to prioritize your own mental health by putting some limits on how you interact with them. Just make sure you communicate those boundaries in a respectful way, so they know it's not about punishing them but about taking care of yourself.

And hey, remember to be gentle with yourself too. Dealing with interpersonal relationships isn't easy, and it's okay to cut yourself some slack as you figure things out.

I hope this helps a bit. And remember, I've always got your back if you need to chat more about this or anything else.

Much love,
Your Aunt

Month End Review

What was new, good, and different about this month?

_____

_____

_____

_____

_____

_____

_____

_____

_____

_____

_____

_____

_____

_____

_____

_____

_____

_____

_____

_____

♡ Fun, fresh, transformational products + services: https://choosebigchange.com ♡

Share Your Vibe

STAY HAPPY (AND COZY) IN STYLE. THE OVERSIZED, DROPPED SHOULDER DESIGN ALLOWS FOR A RELAXED FIT. THIS SWEATSHIRT IS NOT ONLY STYLISH BUT ALSO ECO-CONSCIOUS WHICH MAKES YOU...HAPPY.

ECO FRIENDLY HAPPY SWEATSHIRT

Partnering with Better Cotton to enhance cotton farming worldwide, and made with OEKO-TEX certified low-impact dyes, you can feel good and look even better.

- 80% Ringspun cotton, 20% Polyester (fiber content may vary for different colors) in pink, blue, and gray
- Medium-heavy fabric (8.4 oz/yd² (285 g/m²))
- Classic fit
- Tear-away label

WWW.CHOOSEBIGCHANGE.COM

LUMINOUS MOON DESIGN + PRESS

ASTROLOGY · TAROT · MANIFESTING · NUMEROLOGY

ORACLE CARDS THAT USE THE LANGUAGE OF ASTROLOGY

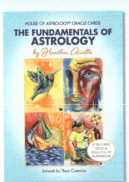

Manifest your heart's desire with 52 beautifully illustrated cards that capture the nuance and duality of each zodiac sign, planet, and house. Use as oracle cards, for spreads, and to learn astrology.

COLOR YOUR OWN TAROT MAJOR ARCANA CARDS

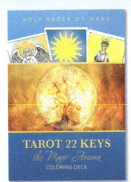

The Tarot Major Arcana represent the Path of Initiation and depict the workings of mind & soul on the Way of Enlightenment. Coloring the cards enables that awareness.

FIND PURPOSE AND PASSION THROUGH MANIFESTATION

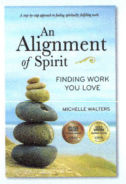

A guide to the inner work necessary for a successful career and all aspects of life using the Manifestation Wheel. Creative activities, manifesting & self-hypnosis.

COMPLETE YOUR NUMEROLOGY CHART

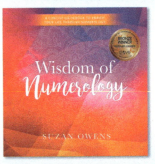

A concise guide to Numerology with quick number reference, definitions, calculations in a nutshell, and blank charts.

Available from Amazon, Barnes & Noble, and wherever books are sold.
Visit our website for more information and to discover more illuminating titles.

LUMINOUSMOON.COM

March

LOOKING AT LEADERSHIP

MARCH 3-9

DO be open and curious.
DO NOT allow self-doubt to creep in.

MARCH 10-16

DO identify where you've been too critical.
DO NOT let your belief systems undermine you.

MARCH 17-23

DO acknowledge the spring equinox.
DO NOT engage with fear of uncertainty.

MARCH 24-30

DO stay true to your authentic self.
DO NOT avoid a month-end review.

WHAT CONSCIOUSNESS CAN I CONTRIBUTE TO THE CHANGING LANDSCAPE OF LEADERSHIP?

MARCH 14, 2:54 AM

FULL MOON LUNAR ECLIPSE
AT 23° VIRGO
NOT EXACTLY PERFECT

MARCH 29, 6:58 AM

NEW MOON SOLAR ECLIPSE
AT 9° ARIES
BRAVE TRANSFORMATION

Energy Almanac 2025 EDITION

♡ Love the Energy Almanac? Tag us on social media: @TheEnergyAlmanac ♡

Month At-A-Glance

◇◇◇

Write in the dates of this month before taking a few minutes to make notes of specific astrological time periods as they intersect with your own life happenings. You may even choose to highlight those time periods in green and red to remind yourself of easy and difficult days.

MONDAY	TUESDAY	WEDNESDAY	THURSDAY	FRIDAY	SATURDAY	SUNDAY

Notes

March

The news March blows in is both practical and bold. It begins with many planets in Aries, the sign of the ram. Your communication style is quick and charismatic early on. Be mindful of aggression. After your clocks "spring ahead" employ the Full Moon Lunar Eclipse in Virgo to bring practical order to your world. Of importance are daily routines and your health. It could be time to let go of old habits that aren't advancing you. March 20 begins the astrological new year and here we grow again. March will wrap up with a stellium in Pisces creating a strong pull toward compassion and creativity. It's a beautiful time to be using your mind's eye to create a vision for yourself and humanity. The warning it comes with is to be mindful of not playing the martyr. Don't limit your dreaming under these strong influences. The eclipse on March 29 concerns leadership and your identity. It's a good time to journal how you'd like to see yourself evolve over the next twelve months. A pivotal moment for humanity occurs on March 30 when Neptune, ruler of faith and imagination, is at zero degrees in its new sign: Aries. For a generation we will witness heart-centered pioneers; leaders who bring with them and encourage compassion, imagination, and spirituality. March is only the beginning of this 20 year transit of Neptune in Aries leaving plenty of time for us to grow into a new way of shepherding. Let's call in love, compassion, strong vision, and faith in all leaders.

TRANSITS

3/1	**Venus Retrograde in Aries**
3/3	**Mercury enters Aries**
3/9	**Daylight Saving Time begins**
3/14	**Full Moon Total Lunar Eclipse at 23° Virgo**
3/15	**Mercury retrograde in Aries**
3/20	**Spring Equinox, Sun enters Aries, Happy birthday, Aries!**
3/20	**International Day of Happiness**
3/27	**Venus Retrograde in Pisces**
3/28	**Stellium: Venus, Mercury & Neptune in Aries**
3/29	**New Moon Partial Solar Eclipse at 9° Aries**
3/29	**Mercury Retrograde in Pisces**
3/30	**Neptune enters Aries**

RESOURCES

Numerology: 3 month in a 9 year

Gemstones: Lapis, Sunstone

Oils: Peppermint, Jasmine

Rituals: Reflect on Your Core Values, Prioritize, Set Boundaries, Listen To Your Intuition

Wisdom Diaries: Authenticity & Integrity

ORACLE PLAY

"What do I need to know about the month ahead?"

CARD 1   CARD 2   CARD 3   CARD 4   CARD 5

_____

_____

_____

_____

_____

♡ Fun, fresh, transformational products + services: https://choosebigchange.com ♡

MARCH PREDICTIONS

MONDAY, MARCH 3 – SUNDAY, MARCH 9	**MOONS:** ARIES, TAURUS, GEMINI, CANCER

March unzips and Mercury, cosmic reporter, enters Aries. Take note as your thoughts and words speed up and are energized, maybe even leaning towards aggression. This transit will be in place the entire month, so be mindful of your words and keep your "I" on the prize of remaining peaceful progress. As the week progresses Taurus, Gemini, and Cancer moons mold our emotions and responses. What are you noticing as the moon makes her moves? More study means is at hand. Research the zodiac signs and use your journal to log information. Thank you Jupiter who is still firmly rooted in Gemini amplifying our curiosity. And before the week closes let's all give three cheers for longer days. On Sunday, daylight savings time begins and we can enjoy more time in the sun. Don't forget to "spring ahead."

GIFT & SHADOW THIS WEEK: *Just one word—Doubt—can tell us so much about the shadow energy for this week. The Sun is in Gate 63-Doubt, which is about using our curiosity to explore ideas and be inspired. However, the shadow plays out here when, instead of doubting what others tell us or what we think is happening, we doubt ourselves, our motivations, and our hearts. The true gift of this week is our experience of silencing the "doubting Thomas" inside our minds and instead being open to new ideas and inspiration triggered by our open curiosity.*

MONDAY, MARCH 10 – SUNDAY, MARCH 16	**MOONS:** LEO, VIRGO, LIBRA

It seems as though learning is a theme, doesn't it, Little Pretzel? Jupiter is expanding curiosity and the Energy Almanac is offering some guidance on how you can amplify your learning of astrology. This week offers the chance to study Leo, Virgo, and Libra before doing some big work around the Full Moon eclipse in Virgo on Friday. Pull out the journal and your laptop so you can research these signs and find the nuances that make them unique. The practical, service-based sign of Virgo is offering you an opportunity to identify where you're being critical and finally release that. Also available is the chance to see where or how your service to others has been dampened. Turn a soft eye on your life and gently assess how your wisdom is valuable to the collective. Look at work routines and health. Let go of what doesn't serve you. The eclipse offers much more! Read our moon article in the resources section.

GIFT & SHADOW THIS WEEK: *Mother Earth challenges us to rise above "stinkin' thinkin'" and create a success mindset this week. The Sun in Gate 22-Grace establishes a pathway to live life from a place of deep love and higher consciousness. Literally, the only things that stand in our way are our patterns of thinking and beliefs that undermine us. I'm not suggesting that you engage in "magical thinking"; instead, observe how you refer to yourself and act when engaged in low-frequency thought patterns. Interrupt the pattern by inserting positive words of encouragement, and watch how you transform.*

✳ Get your book bonus offers: www.choosebigchange.com/pages/bonus25 ✳

| MONDAY, MARCH 17 – SUNDAY, MARCH 23 | **MOONS:** LIBRA, SCORPIO, SAGITTARIUS, CAPRICORN |

Forewarned is fore-armed. This week you get to chill and study and study and chill before next week's big transits occur. For now, keep your eye on the moon as it moves from Libra through Capricorn. Journal out, pen in hand, compare this week's energy to the week of February 17-23. You should start to notice patterns. Check again against January 20-26. Here is where you can really begin to understand how you personally relate to astrology. Once again, we should all thank Jupiter in Gemini for encouraging this edification process. March 20 the sun enters Aries and the astrological new year begins. The Spring Equinox is time to acknowledge a season of new beginnings and the planting of seeds. What will you grow in the year ahead? It's also International Day of Happiness. Your work is to find multiple reasons to notice joy. In the Tibetan tradition you can "smile from your liver." Be sure to tag us in your post on social media. We are @TheEnergyAlmanac.

GIFT & SHADOW THIS WEEK: *Saturn and the Sun move into Gate 36-Turbulence this week. We may be having a severe collective or personal "dark night of the Soul." There is uncertainty in the world—a feeling of disaster or the other shoe about to drop, leading us to emotional turmoil. Last year, it was Neptune sitting at this Gate. We learned that tuning into our inner self and higher spiritual consciousness helped us move through trying times. We tap into the Gift this week and this year when we create foundations that support humanity with love and compassion. Remember, it begins with how you treat yourself.*

FUN, FRESH, TRANSFORMATIONAL COMPANION PRODUCTS TO HELP MAKE 2025 AMAZING ARE AVAILABLE AT:

WWW.CHOOSEBIGCHANGE.COM

Energy Almanac 2025 Edition

Page 57

MONDAY, MARCH 24 – SUNDAY, MARCH 30

MOONS: CAPRICORN, AQUARIUS, PISCES

Finally the big work is in front of us. This week's astrology is coming at you from Venus, Mercury, and Neptune, as well as the Moon. The week is back-loaded with transits. You have Monday and Tuesday to plan and use your intuition to guide the potentials happening astrologically. Wednesday hosts Venus moving retrograde in the sign of Pisces. Your big loving heart can be feeling rather soft and self-love work can be amplified if you will not wallow too long. It's an extremely good time to look inward. Flavor the Venus retrograde with Mercury retrograde and Neptune retrograde in Pisces and you have the perfect time for a deeply transformational experience with spirit. This stellium, collection of planets in one sign, highlights Pisces traits. Spirituality, compassion, love, creativity, vision, intuition all collide intellectually, inside of relationships, value systems, and across generations. It's a cosmic moment meant to bring attention to big love and to shine that light upon, not just our neighbors, but on ourselves, too. It's a perfect day to host a group meditation, self-love study, or vision boarding day for lasting impact. The Saturday solar eclipse in Aries is a powerful start to the new astrological year. Be sure to read the moon article on page 61. Adding to its potency is the fact that Neptune, the planet of faith and love, lies in its final degree. Often referred to as a karmic degree, what happens on and around this day will move with us for a long while. On Sunday, Neptune, our powerful grandfather figure, will move into zero degrees of Aries foretelling a massive shift in spiritual consciousness that is too big to be described here. Read the front of the book section titled "Important Planetary Moves" before moving on. It's on pages 12-13. Let's just say that this week is one for the books. You'll want to make many notes in your journal about what is happening in the outer landscape as well as what is going on in your personal world. Don't forget your month end review process. Check on your quarterly progress, too. It might be time to adjust your strategy before sending second quarter goals.

GIFT & SHADOW THIS WEEK: *The planet Uranus moves into Gate 8-Contribution this week. Uranus as the planet of awakening tends to create a situation where we must seek to express our personal authenticity. In Gate 8, we tend to shut down our individuality in favor of "fitting in" which means we are all not quite sure who we are. The result is that from now through July 9, 2025 we might find ourselves struggling to identify and take action on our personal dreams. The struggle will encourage us to break out of and break through any barriers to being our true selves. Inside every person is a genius—your job is to find yours and live it out loud!*

_____
_____
_____
_____
_____
_____
_____
_____
_____
_____

March Moon Work

MARCH 14, 2:54 AM FULL MOON LUNAR ECLIPSE AT 23° VIRGO	 NOT EXACTLY PERFECT

March comes in like a lion and the Full Moon lunar eclipse in Virgo adds a mighty cosmic roar to the season. Your intuition is still dropping insights into your days and your emotions are high as revelations about your worthiness pop-in. The planets have a plan to continue to feed you information, some of which could be revelatory! Creativity and imagination could be useful if you will bear down and be practical in your application and use of the insights that are coming your way. It's possible you could feel confused by your imaginings or feel a need to tighten your relationship with Source. That doesn't mean you should be critical of yourself for the confusion, use it as a reminder to slow down and employ the right timing of your deeds.

You may notice connections between your intuitive hits and a deep soulfulness as it relates to your own acts of service (Virgo) and leadership (Chiron in Aries). Should you choose to act (Mars) on any of it, be sure your gut gives you the big "Heck yes." As fast and furious as information is coming be sure to apply pragmatic thinking to your ideas. And remember, nobody is perfect, so allow yourself to see all the good in all you've done.

Virgo is ultimately about being industrious and productive, practical and exacting all in the name of service. Holistic in nature, it's also a good time to let go of old habits that are unhealthy and ask your higher self to share what might be better choices that would improve your life force.

AFFIRMATION: *"I know and trust what is coming to me and release what doesn't serve."*

MOON WORK:

- Determine how you can be practical about changing how you see yourself. What steps can you take to initiate positive self-worth without criticizing yourself?
- Write a prayer of release regarding your health, invite in new healthy habits.
- When making your decisions under this moon, use list-making of pros and cons as a sensible way to sort through the topic.

_____

_____

_____

_____

_____

_____

_____

_____

♡ Fun, fresh, transformational products + services: https://choosebigchange.com ♡

MARCH 29, 6:58 AM
NEW MOON SOLAR ECLIPSE AT 9° ARIES

BRAVE TRANSFORMATION

Eclipses come in pairs. This New Moon solar eclipse is in the initiating sign of the ram. It's also the first moon of the astrological new year and begins an entirely new cycle. Dreams and goals set under this energy will flavor the twelve months ahead so pay careful attention. Happily, the Sun and Moon are shoulder-to-shoulder with Mercury today and the energy is dynamic and reactive if you aren't careful. With such brusque energy stay mindful about thinking before you speak. Going through you are plenty of soul-fueled emotions and a passion for creativity which could help to soften anything too impulsive.

Mars in Cancer is holding hands with Venus in Pisces and the dance is on between deep emotion and big creativity. Use your intuition and big heart inside of relationships at this time. You'll be feeling all the feels while working to maintain your autonomy.

The higher and lower minds are united in setting up a vision for you; though it may be murky now, if you follow the breadcrumbs, you will likely notice an area of life that is transforming and where your future self will benefit. Don't forget that as you change, you add to the collective transformation (Pluto in Aquarius), so don't be afraid to let your intuition lead you to greater things. Dream big under this new moon.

AFFIRMATION: *"I am bold, brave, and ready to lead my own transformation."*

MOON WORK:

- Find where Aquarius is in your natal birth chart, this will help you understand which area of your life is changing over the next many years. Locate which house it is in then Google what life area that house number is about.
- Set a goal for what you want to be, do, and have over the next twelve months.
- Research the "Tower" card to understand the archetype of Aries energy.

_____
_____
_____
_____
_____
_____
_____
_____
_____
_____
_____
_____

Numerology

Numerologically this is a three month in a nine year.
March = 3 and 2025 = 9; 3 + 9 = 12; 1 + 2 = 3

Three is the number of creativity and expression. It's a matter of optimism, too. You may notice this force under-pinning this month. It's a playful feeling perfect for softening the Aries energy that is so prevalent.

Gemstones & Oils

GEMSTONES

Lapis Activates third eye and throat chakra, brings inner peace, enhances wisdom and insight, clears emotional baggage and expectations, and allows one to honestly be themselves.

Sunstone Wise leadership, heightens happiness, inspires freedom and motivation simultaneously, clears negative and critical thinking while welcoming abundance and optimism.

OILS

Peppermint *Mentha x piperita*
Visionary, attentive, optimistic, leadership
Blends well w/ Lemon, Orange, Rose, Pine, Rosemary

Peppermint's invigorating, optimistic nature opens the mind and allows digestion of thoughts to occur, leaving you with focused, confident and fearless energy to implement new ideas. Peppermint has leadership qualities allowing information to come in and be put into action without your personal emotions taking over your decisions. It is helpful when emotional tolerance is needed to handle issues. Peppermint is the oil of the people. Think of it as the unforgettable charismatic guest at the party that leaves everyone feeling heard, valued, appreciated and liked, all with just their friendly smile, sturdy handshake and good listening skills.

Jasmine *Jasminum grandiflorum*
Fearless, bold, creative
Blends well w/ Sandalwood, Orange, Vanilla, Bergamot, Vetiver, Patchouli

Jasmine is useful to ignite the fertility of the mind. She knocks down barriers left and right by removing self doubt and thoughts of inadequacy. She takes your ideas of passion and creativity and boldly dances with you on the dance floor helping you bring these creations into real life. She evokes the spirit of daringly bold play.

_____

_____

_____

♡ Fun, fresh, transformational products + services: https://choosebigchange.com ♡

Rhythms, Routines & Rituals

Grab a journal and noodle on these ideas to embrace this month's energy of self-leadership.

- **Reflect on Your Core Values:** Self-leadership begins with your values. What values are most important to you? Examples might be adventure, service, compassion, family, health, personal growth...the list is endless. Get clear on yours.

- **Prioritize:** What are the top three to five values that you consider non-negotiable? These are the principles that you are not willing to compromise on, regardless of the circumstances and will help you to stay true to yourself. This is also a stellar tool for decision making.

- **Set Boundaries:** What boundaries align with your non-negotiables? For example, if you have identified family as a value, and want connect with family over dinner, then a boundary may be no devices at the table so that everyone can be present.

- **Listen To Your Intuition:** Your gut knows what's what. Pay attention to your gut feelings and instincts. If something doesn't feel aligned, trust your intuition as a valuable guide. Energy testing is my go to for this.

Not having clear values, boundaries, and priorities is like trying to drive cross country without a GPS. You may get there, eventually, but with a lot of stress and wrong turns. Putting these practices into place will allow for a much smoother ride through March. To start creating your value-based life, grab my bonus material.

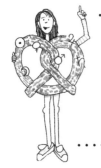

WANT EVEN MORE ROOM TO WRITE? GET THE MATCHING ENERGY ALMANAC JOURNAL FOR CAPTURING ALL OF YOUR THOUGHTS.

GO TO CHOOSEBIGCHANGE.COM AND TYPE IN "JOURNAL" TO SEE OUR AVAILABLE COLLECTION. WE HAVE LOTS TO CHOOSE FROM!

� Get your book bonus offers: www.choosebigchange.com/pages/bonus25 ✧

Wisdom Diaries

Hey Grandpa,

I hope you're doing well. I've been thinking a lot about what it really means to be a good leader. People are looking to me more and more for advice or to solve problems and give clarity but sometimes I still feel like I don't know what I am doing. I want to step up and help hold some of the responsibility for the growth of my community...so, who better to turn to for guidance on this than you?

You've always been the epitome of a compassionate and wise leader, both in our family and in the community. Your ability to really listen, empathize with others, and lead with integrity has always been something I've looked up to. You are truly inspiring.

As I start thinking about how I can embody these same qualities in my own life, I'd love to hear your thoughts on how to be a more heart-centered leader. What kind of daily practices can I start incorporating to lead with authenticity and integrity? And how do you deal with the inevitable roadblocks and setbacks that come with leadership while still staying true to your heart-centered values?

Your wisdom and advice mean the world to me as I navigate this journey towards becoming a better leader, for myself and for my community. Thanks for always being there for me with your guidance, inspiration, and unconditional love.

> With all my respect and gratitude,
> Your Grandchild

Hey there,

Wow, I gotta say, your honesty and maturity in reaching out for advice really impresses me. It means a lot that I'm thrilled to hear that you're diving into the world of leadership and aiming to bring authenticity and integrity to the table. Those qualities are cornerstone to our family's values, and they really hold the foundation when it comes to making a positive impact on the folks you lead and the world around you.

Being authentic means being true to yourself, flaws and all, and leading with honesty and transparency. It takes guts to show up as your real self, especially in a world where fitting in often seems more important than standing out. But trust me, true leadership starts with authenticity. People are more likely to follow someone who's genuine and straight-forward.

To get your authenticity game strong, start by figuring out what really matters to you. What gets you out of bed in the morning? What do you believe in, deep down? Let those values guide your decisions and actions as a leader. And don't be afraid to show your human side—it's okay to admit when you don't have all the answers.

Integrity is another biggie in the leadership world. It's all about walking the talk, even when nobody's watching. Doing the right thing, even when it's tough, builds trust and respect—two things every leader needs in spades. Be honest, be accountable, and treat everyone with fairness and respect, no matter who they are.

And remember, leadership isn't about bossing people around—it's about lifting them up and helping them shine. Lead with humility, empathy, and kindness, and watch as your authenticity and integrity inspire others to do the same.

I know you're going to be an amazing leader, one who leads from the heart and makes a real difference in people's lives. Keep being true to yourself and sticking to your values—you've got this.

> Lots of love and support,
> Grandpa

♡ Fun, fresh, transformational products + services: https://choosebigchange.com ♡

Month End Review

◇ ◈ ◇

What was new, good, and different about this month?

_____
_____
_____
_____
_____
_____
_____
_____
_____
_____
_____
_____
_____
_____
_____
_____
_____
_____
_____
_____
_____
_____

April

APPLYING SENSIBLE SOLUTIONS

MARCH 31–APRIL 6

DO pour on the self-love this week.
DO NOT avoid regulating your responses.

APRIL 7–13

DO practice your leadership skills.
DO NOT become fearful about the future.

APRIL 14–20

DO make a list of ways you can have fun.
DO NOT be harsh during self-observation.

APRIL 21–27

DO notice where you can get more "in flow."
DO NOT avoid self-love practices.

APRIL 28–MAY 4

DO pay attention to sudden insights.
DO NOT avoid a month-end review.

WHAT ARE THE GREATEST POSSIBILITIES AVAILABLE TO ME NOW?

APRIL 12, 8:22 PM

FULL MOON AT 23° LIBRA
PASSIONATE & PROPER PARTNERSHIPS

APRIL 27, 3:31 PM

NEW MOON AT 7° TAURUS
CREATING A NEW POINT OF VIEW

Energy Almanac 2025 Edition

Month At-A-Glance

Write in the dates of this month before taking a few minutes to make notes of specific astrological time periods as they intersect with your own life happenings. You may even choose to highlight those time periods in green and red to remind yourself of easy and difficult days.

MONDAY	TUESDAY	WEDNESDAY	THURSDAY	FRIDAY	SATURDAY	SUNDAY

Notes

April

With the fresh air of April here you can trust that underground roots are growing just like the dreams you planted at the spring equinox last month. While early in the month lessons in spirituality work with the economy we can all use our extremely active imaginations to press sensible solutions into the economic atmosphere. Early on Pisces energy is strong again as a stellium forms in the firmament bringing with it more compassion, more creativity, and more imagination. If only you could get paid for daydreaming! Mid month seems energetic with both Aries and Leo fire energy but don't get too comfortable with that jubilance because when the Sun moves into Taurus on the 19th we become more grounded and things slow a bit. April 21 holds a transit that recruits right timing, discipline, structure and loving and dreaming. These odd bedfellows are making friends and you can find yourself asking how a more controlled and creative approach to fantasizing could help everyone. The New moon is on the 27th in the earthy sign of Taurus and it's okay to set your sights on improving your personal resources.

TRANSITS

4/2	**International Fact Checking Day**
4/5	**Stellium: Saturn, Venus, Mercury all in Pisces**
4/7	**Mercury direct in Pisces**
4/12	**Full Moon at 23° Libra,** read moon article
4/12	**Venus direct in Pisces**
4/16	**Mercury enters Aries**
4/18	**Mars enters Leo**
4/19	**Sun enters Taurus, Happy birthday, Taurians**
4/21	**Saturn conjunct North Node**
4/27	**New Moon at 7° Taurus,** read moon article
4/30	**Venus enters Aries**

RESOURCES

Numerology: 4 month in a 9 year

Gemstones: Garnet, Blue Lace Agate

Oils: Cypress, Lavender

Rituals: Gratitude Journaling, Learn To Say No, Connect With Loved Ones, Continuous Learning, Digital Detox

Wisdom Diaries: Balance & Detachment

ORACLE PLAY

"What do I need to know about the month ahead?"

CARD 1   CARD 2   CARD 3   CARD 4   CARD 5

_____

_____

_____

_____

_____

♡ Fun, fresh, transformational products + services: https://choosebigchange.com ♡

APRIL PREDICTIONS

MONDAY, MARCH 31 – SUNDAY, APRIL 6	MOONS: TAURUS, GEMINI, CANCER

Wow. Yesterday Neptune entered the karmic zero degree point in Aries and we collectively began a long journey of heart-centered leadership. It's an incredible time to be alive, Little Pretzel. Make strong notes of what you notice this week in the area of compassionate leadership; it's a foretelling. Wednesday is the perfect day for research! Not only is it ruled by Mercury, our logical thinker, but it's also International Fact Checking Day. In other astrological news April fourth brings some intensity to potential thoughts or discussion about the spiritual potentials of the changing economy. A serious approach to compassion and the changing landscape of the outer economy or inner self-worth could trigger your emotions. Pour on the self-love. Saturday is a second stellium or cluster of planets in the sign of Pisces, meant to trigger the amplification of boundless visions of a loving, compassionate society. What can you contribute to the dream?

GIFT & SHADOW THIS WEEK: *The shadow energies of control and inadequacy are what we are working on through this week. While we may be struggling with our need to control or being controlled by others, this week's truth is that we are only responsible for regulating ourselves. However, there is a much larger shadow/gift looming for us, and it's activated for an extended period, which makes me think it will be background noise for a long time this year.*

We begin April with Venus, Mercury, the North Node, and Saturn all at Gate 36-Crisis. The inner planets Venus and Mercury make this a personal shadow, the North Node is a collective consciousness trajectory, and Saturn presents us with the social and cultural changes happening around us. The central theme of this shadow is moving us from crisis to humanity and compassion. There will likely be emotional volatility all around us, yet if we learn to stay in our compassionate hearts, we can move through this turbulence and change our culture to be more caring and humanitarian. It's a big ask but one we are well suited to achieve.

MONDAY, APRIL 7 – SUNDAY, APRIL 13	MOONS: LEO, VIRGO, LIBRA

The second week of April offers the opportunity to just be in leadership and own your identity. Monday opens with World Health Day. Kick off the week with your commitment to improving your well being. Outside of that, with the sun positioned in Aries you showing up as you are innately felt. Practice that this week before Saturday's Full Moon in Libra which is about relationships and balance. The co-conspirator of Aries "I" energy is Libra's "WE" energy. What are they conspiring on? Your personal growth. The Full Moon suggests coupling, legalities, peace, money, and self-worth. Get deep instruction by reading the article in this month's resources section on page 71.

GIFT & SHADOW THIS WEEK: *We continue the awakening and consciousness-raising energy this week with the Sun at Gate 51-Shock. Most people fear change, and the Sun at this Gate reminds us that change is the name of the game on planet Earth. There may also be triggers in the outer world that make us fearful about the future. Truthfully, you are well-equipped to move with ease and grace through all life's experiences by staying "in-tune" with your intuition and instinct.*

✳ Get your book bonus offers: www.choosebigchange.com/pages/bonus25 ✳

MONDAY, APRIL 14 – SUNDAY, APRIL 20

MOONS: SCORPIO, SAGITTARIUS, CAPRICORN

Take a deep breath, Little Pretzel, this week's astrology has a lot to manage. It all starts on Wednesday when Mercury, planetary communicator, enters Aries and your words are fired up. There's a new intensity and passion behind what you're saying for the next few weeks. Watch for impatience under this influence, too. Friday brings Mars in Leo and your strength and determination begin to amplify. Mars could have you singing and dancing through life for a few weeks or perhaps romantic overtures turn up. Certainly there will be much more fun and enthusiasm to handle. Make a list of all the ways you can have more fun through mid-June. Sunday Funday arrives and the Sun himself pulls on the denim overalls of earthy, slow-moving, tradition loving Taurus. Belly up to the board as you become more tactile and resourceful for the next month. The subconscious influences are so interesting, aren't they? What are you noticing about yourself now?

GIFT & SHADOW THIS WEEK: *What is success? What is failure? We may be struggling with these two energies this week. We all have ambitions, dreams, and goals, and how do you judge yourself in realizing those aspirations? If we are harsh in our judgment of success or failure, we may totally miss the lesson involved in the experience. Celebrate all your experiences as they are filled with truths you want to learn.*

_____

_____

_____

MONDAY, APRIL 21 – SUNDAY, APRIL 27

MOONS: AQUARIUS, PISCES, ARIES

Grab a box of tissue and your favorite prayer book friend because Saturn is standing hip-to-hip with the lunar north node on Monday. The next seven days are flavored with compassion, and creativity. Your work is to notice where you can apply flow. How can you break boundaries and lean into boundless dreaming for yourself and society? Saturn applies pressure but Pisces dreams have no limits. The North Node encourages you to move in the direction of those unlimited possibilities with a big, loving heart. As the planetary transit wanes toward the end of the week note the dynamic Aries energy presented by the Moon herself. With big limitless dreams, how can you be more courageous? That's one for your journal! Also for your journal is the New Moon in Taurus which addresses resources and values. Sunday reread the moon article in this month's holistic resources.

GIFT & SHADOW THIS WEEK: *Celebrate through releasing fear—Yay! We are nearing the end of the Earth's transit through the Gates of the Spleen in our Human Designs. The Gates on the Spleen Center can double as fear and paralysis points for us. Most of all our shadows and fears would disappear if we were to do one thing first: practice self-care and self-love. Life really is an adventure, and we are the drivers. When we make decisions that come from healthy self-centeredness, we find ourselves in the right place, at the right time, with the right opportunities. So enjoy life, face your fears, and celebrate moving ahead fearlessly!*

_____

_____

_____

♡ Fun, fresh, transformational products + services: https://choosebigchange.com ♡

MONDAY, APRIL 28 – SUNDAY, MAY 4	**MOONS:** TAURUS, GEMINI, CANCER

April is winding down this week but will go out with a little flair when Venus enters Aries. Venus is the cosmic Marilyn Monroe, all love, money, and beauty while Aries is represented by the football uniform, ready for action. Here we enjoy passionate coupling with an individualistic intensity attached. You may feel driven to have more pleasure and go after what you desire. Wednesday is a good day for your month-end review if you haven't done it already. Set your goals during some downtime this weekend. Sunday Uranus, planet of revelation, in the sign of Taurus, using a sextile, tickles the lunar north node in Pisces. Sextiles are benevolent transits. You may get some sudden insights about using your resources to help you reach your dreams. You might get intuitive hits about how to turn on the self-love and own your true value. As always, capture the information in your journal for this year.

GIFT & SHADOW THIS WEEK: *This week's energy focuses on purpose, allowing, and fulfillment. Purpose is tricky because we can fall into a trap of constantly seeking our purpose and potentially feeling like a failure if we don't find it or live it out. Instead, realize that when you follow your passion, your life is a blank canvas, and you're the artist. The art of allowing is built on trust and faith in your worthiness to have help along the way. We learn that no one is an island and that we all need each other to reach the highest states of abundance, love, and support.*

_____

_____

April Moon Work

APRIL 12, 8:22 PM		PASSIONATE & PROPER
FULL MOON AT 23° LIBRA		PARTNERSHIPS

Partnership may be the mighty force of the full moon that flavors this day but don't discount the zeal for staying in your shell. The sun and moon are tense against Mars making this an emotional day for relations. Your loyalty is fierce and you have thoughts and feelings that are apt to ramp up your temperament as well. As your curiosity piques, ask questions of your Higher Self and try to intuit the answers that arise concerning your collaborators. The disciplined approach could help intuit answers. It is interesting how Mars in Cancer is influencing 7 celestial bodies and Mercury in the artist's smock of Pisces is playing with six. You personally will feel the tug of your sixth sense and passionate loyalty toward the sanctuary of your home life. Mars in Cancer can be moody, so stay alert to not being passive aggressive today. The intellect and the higher mind are working hard under this moon, so let's give grace where needed.

Also of extreme importance under this full Moon is Neptune's position. Neptune is aspected by four planets which is likely to induce some confusion. Venus, Mars, Mercury and Saturn all have something to whisper to the keeper of wisdom, Neptune. The vision will clear but you must employ compassion and faith wherever possible as the mystery unfolds.

The north node is also actively tickling your subconscious mind and urging you towards bold moves. Be sure to time those carefully.

AFFIRMATION: *"I am attracting all of the right people, resources and opportunities I need."*

MOON WORK:

- Review your partnerships at work and home, see who or what you can leave behind.
- Check yourself before you wreck yourself. Assume you are the partner that is in the wrong, journal a version of yourself that you'd like to present to the world.
- Discover which house your natal Cancer is in your chart. Find the house then Google it to discover in which life area you are currently feeling more bold and dynamic.

_____

_____

_____

_____

_____

_____

_____

♡ Fun, fresh, transformational products + services: https://choosebigchange.com ♡

APRIL 27, 3:31 PM
NEW MOON AT 7° TAURUS

 # CREATING A NEW POINT OF VIEW

This mid-spring moon has the two luminaries squaring Mars in Leo flavoring your mind with creative activity. There are thoughts of the changing group dynamics that come into play but really, it's slow and steady that wins the race, so be your practical self as you dream today. Playing with clay and forming things with your hands is a good use of the creative energy that builds under this moon and as you get into flow set the intention to capture the ideas that are sure to come in waves. Expand the vision and offer it with faith to Source.

Your imagination is strong and useful as a tool for manifestation however Taurus is practical. Using your imagination and creativity to build your own self-worth as well as to develop new streams of income could be a valuable way to spend time. It's entirely possible that the business you've been wanting to build that will serve the changing landscape of humanity will be born under this beautiful lunation.

If questions of whether or not you are capable of being a solid leader crop up, disregard them. Today it is a new moon and a new point of view.

AFFIRMATION: *"I am worthy of a life I love."*

MOON WORK:

- Taurus is about money, resources, and values. Do a review of your budget and resources to discover your net worth then create a goal to grow that number.
- Earthy creativity is called for! Make something using found items from the Earth. Pick up sticks, stones, leaves, clay, and more to build a collage.
- Meditate on the topic of "self-worth" and imagine yourself with the full confidence that you deserve the best of everything.

_____
_____
_____
_____
_____
_____
_____
_____
_____
_____
_____
_____

Numerology

Numerologically this is a four month in a nine year.
April = 4 and 2025 = 9; 4 + 9 = 13; 1 + 3 = 4

Four is a foundational number which gives you the opportunity to put legs under anything you've desired. Its energy is for planning and adding structure to your goals. Use the wisdom of the nine year to do tasks with time-tested knowledge supporting it.

Gemstones & Oils

GEMSTONES

Garnet This regenerative stone strengthens memory and focus, invites self love and primal love to the forefront, protects against evil and negativity, and calms the heart in crisis.

Blue Lace Agate Promotes confidence, peace, forgiveness, calmness, open communication, stabilizes the energy field, and alleviates anger, anxiety, and stress.

OILS

Cypress *Cupressus sempervirens*
Transitions, leading, clarity, intuitive
Blends well w/ Rosemary, Cedarwood, Lavender

Cypress oil assists times of transitions offering a strong command to find solutions for all challenges. Cypress' direct nature allows focused messages from source to come through clearly. It is useful when making practical decisions.

Lavender *Lavandoula angustifolia*
Sensible, nurturing, calm composure
Blends well w/ Rose, Grapefruit, Cedarwood, Rosemary

Like a mother, Lavender is known for her sensible, compassionate nurturing. Lavender brings harmony to the chakras encouraging balance and calmness to make reasonable changes and choices while keeping you grounded. When siblings rival it is the calm asserting motherly nature of Lavender that is able to bring ease in self expression all while feeling supported.

_____
_____
_____
_____
_____

♡ Fun, fresh, transformational products + services: https://choosebigchange.com ♡

Rhythms, Routines & Rituals

Practicing self-love is like a big cozy hug and it's crucial to get into the flow of this month's energies for supporting your overall well-being. Try these habits for a boost of self-love:

- **Gratitude Journaling:** Keep a gratitude journal to reflect on all the positive aspects of your life. Consider the big things, like family and health, or small gifts like the tree in your yard, or your morning coffee. I swap my list with a friend every day to stay accountable.

- **Learn To Say No:** Say no to things that don't align with your well-being or values. Prioritize your time and energy for activities that fill your cup. If it's not a heck yes, it's probably a no. No is a complete sentence, no explanation needed.

- **Connect With Loved Ones:** Pick up the phone or plan a coffee date to nurture relationships with friends and family.

- **Continuous Learning:** Be a lifelong student. Whether it's taking up a new hobby, reading a book or attending workshops, knowledge is fuel for the soul.

- **Digital Detox:** Unplug from electronic devices and social media. Taking time away allows you to spend time on relationships, health, hobbies, not to mention better sleep. Even your devices need time to recharge!.

Try these habits on for size and see what fits, and be patient with yourself as you learn to show yourself some love. Grab my bonus material for practical solutions to finding your rhythm.

_____

_____

_____

_____

_____

_____

_____

_____

_____

_____

GET YOUR FREE BONUS CONTENT AT:
WWW.CHOOSEBIGCHANGE.COM/PAGES/BONUS25

Scan here

Hey Uncle,

Hope you're doing well. With spring rolling in, I've been doing some thinking about finding balance and staying grounded, especially when it comes to making big decisions and planning for the future. And who better to turn to for some wisdom on this than you?

You've always been someone I look up to for your steadiness and level-headedness, both in your personal and professional life. The way you handle challenges with such calm and resilience is seriously impressive. I admire how you manage to keep your cool and hold onto your dignity even when life gets chaotic.

So, I'm curious—how do you do it? How do you approach decision-making and planning for the future in a way that keeps you balanced and clear-headed? What tricks do you have up your sleeve for quieting the noise and tapping into your inner wisdom before making big choices?

And speaking of balance, how do you find that sweet spot between being proactive and patient? How do you set goals and chase your dreams while still staying open to unexpected opportunities and changes in direction?

Your insights would mean the world to me as I try to navigate my own journey through life. Thanks for always being there with your wisdom, inspiration, and unconditional support

Catch you later,
Your Niece/Nephew

Hey there,

I'm glad you reached out, and I'm happy to share some thoughts on finding balance and making decisions.

When it comes to practicing the pause, I've found that taking a step back and giving myself some breathing room before making big choices can really make a difference. Whether it's going for a walk, meditating, or just taking a few deep breaths, finding a way to clear your head can help you tap into your inner wisdom. Ask Spirit to show you the path of least resistance, or a few of the best options when making life decisions. Remember, Creator holds the highest perspective and always wants what is best for you.

As for striking a balance between being proactive and patient, it's all about finding that middle ground. I like to set goals and make plans, but I also try to stay flexible and open to new opportunities. Sometimes life throws unexpected curveballs, and being able to roll with the punches is just as important as having a game plan.

Hope that helps a bit. Remember, finding balance is a journey, not a destination, so don't be too hard on yourself if things don't always go according to plan.

Take care,
Your Uncle

April

Month End Review
◇◇◇

What was new, good, and different about this month?

May

DREAM THE IMPOSSIBLE DREAM

MAY 5–11

DO trust in the divine unfolding.
DO NOT discount a higher power.

MAY 12–18

DO be compassionate as often as possible.
DO NOT contribute until the time is right.

MAY 19–25

DO explore new ideas for educating yourself.
DO NOT worry about having enough resources.

MAY 26–JUNE 1

DO only say yes to the right opportunities.
DO NOT avoid a month-end review.

WHAT CAN I CHOOSE TO BE MORE OF ME?

MAY 12, 12:56 PM

FULL MOON AT 22° SCORPIO
THE MYSTERIES OF MONEY

MAY 26, 11:02 PM

NEW MOON AT 6° GEMINI
CURIOUS ABOUT LEADING

Energy Almanac 2025 Edition

Month At-A-Glance

Write in the dates of this month before taking a few minutes to make notes of specific astrological time periods as they intersect with your own life happenings. You may even choose to highlight those time periods in green and red to remind yourself of easy and difficult days.

MONDAY	TUESDAY	WEDNESDAY	THURSDAY	FRIDAY	SATURDAY	SUNDAY

 Notes

May

It seems like all the planets have wanted to play with the North Node in Pisces early this year. In May, right out of the gate, Uranus is having a tryst with it. Uranus is in Taurus creating change in the economy and the Universe is envisioning a compassionate use of finances. Later, Jupiter is in its final degrees of Gemini, the cosmic scholar, and he's creating movement in leaders and expanding the vision of how we educate. It's a spectacular time in human history that we now get to create lasting change. In May you may be led to do your own deep work. Don't be afraid of getting curious as to what that might look like and do use your imagination to go further than you thought. Dare to dream the impossible dream. Toward the end of the month you may feel quite social and curious with all of the planets that are in Gemini. Roll with it. Gather and chatter knowing you are "under the influence."

TRANSITS

5/4	**Pluto Retrograde in Aquarius**
5/6	**International No Diet Day**
5/10	**Mercury enters Taurus**
5/12	**Full Moon at 22° Scorpio,** read moon article
5/20	**Sun enters Gemini, Happy birthday, Gemini!**
5/24	**Saturn enters Aries**
5/25	**Mercury enters Gemini**
5/26	**New Moon at 6° Gemini,** read moon article

RESOURCES

Numerology: 5 month in a 9 year

Gemstones: Moldavite, Dendritic Agate

Oils: Clary Sage, Nutmeg

Rituals: Vision Board Creation, Morning Visualization, Goal Setting and Planning, Daily Affirmations

Wisdom Diaries: Imagination & Creativity

ORACLE PLAY

"What do I need to know about the month ahead?"

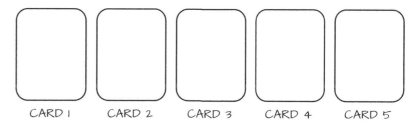

CARD 1   CARD 2   CARD 3   CARD 4   CARD 5

_____

_____

_____

_____

♡ Fun, fresh, transformational products + services: https://choosebigchange.com ♡

MAY PREDICTIONS

MONDAY, MAY 5 – SUNDAY, MAY 11	MOONS: LEO, VIRGO, LIBRA

The Sun is already in the earthy tradition-loving sign of Taurus and on Saturday Mercury will enter the sign as well. The next few weeks offer you a good opportunity to scrutinize your budget. Separately, you may investigate your level of self-worth with a deep understanding of "your net worth is often equivalent to your self-worth." What generative experience could you have by simply loving yourself more? Good news! Tuesday is International No Diet Day. If you were hoping to have reason to eat a second helping, this is your excuse. In other news, the moon will be in the sign of Taurus over the weekend, too, giving more energy to the personal investigation of these topics. It's may. Go to a garden or a walking trail, take off your shoes and get grounded. Taurus love the dirt. Put your hands on the Earth and ask "How can I love myself more?" Allow yourself to be surprised and delighted by the answers.

GIFT & SHADOW THIS WEEK: *Saturn, the planet of discipline and responsibility, moves into Gate 25-Spirit this week. This week's challenge and lesson is to trust in Divine Order in your life. Without trust in a higher power, we can get caught in constriction, feeling like we have no choices or that the world is against us. However, that is never true. We are all sparks of the divine and have consistent access to higher consciousness. All we have to do is trust our instinctual awareness and move toward fulfilling our Divine Purpose.*

MONDAY, MAY 12 – SUNDAY, MAY 18	MOONS: SCORPIO, SAGITTARIUS, CAPRICORN

All Mondays are moon days, but this Monday is the Full Moon in Scorpio which brings a big mystery to this spring-time event. Your transformation is at hand and you can use this transit fully by leaning into the instructions in our moon article this month. The rest of the planetary action happens on Sunday, so hold onto your panties as we walk you through this. Jupiter, the cosmic cheerleader, is in some of its final degrees of Gemini. It's been expanding our curiosity and learning. It's been questioning education. It is going to square off against the collective sacred wound, Chiron, in Aries. Jupiter will also square off against the North Node (karmic collective destiny) in Pisces and that North Node will semi-sextile the sacred wound. To bring it down to nuts and bolts, there are questions or learning to be done about how you individually can contribute to the greater good through your own autonomy and individualism. The answer lies somewhere between adding compassion as often as possible and visioning yourself a grand leader, secure in who you are. Enjoy the process of asking and answering your own questions about this. Write three things you can contribute to healing the current world wound concerning leadership, individualism, and being more brave. For extra points, share it on social media and tag us @TheEnergyAlmanac.

GIFT & SHADOW THIS WEEK: *We all want to be heard, seen, valued, and recognized for our genius, but often we end up sharing information at the wrong time and people look at us as if we have sprouted two heads! This week's gift is about you sharing your brilliance in the right time, with the right people. That means learning when it is appropriate to share and when it isn't. When is it appropriate? It is appropriate when you have been invited to share your insights. Slow down the process of sharing long enough to know whether those who hear your words will value what you have to say.*

MONDAY, MAY 19 – SUNDAY, MAY 25	MOONS: AQUARIUS, PISCES, ARIES

This week presents us with a societal shift sure to be felt across the planet but before that, on Monday, the Sun enters Aries and we salute all those born under this influence. You are bold and charismatic; you are a leader. If you're not born an Aries while the Sun is in this zodiac you may notice yourself taking more action and being in general more dynamic. Take note of this in your journal to see if it's true for you. Saturday societal planet and cosmic grandfather Saturn enters the sign of Aries. This journey brings about pressure to leaders everywhere. It's the opportunity to bring order and structure to our actions and to take leadership seriously. Read more about this two year transit in the article titled "Important Planetary Moves" at the front of this book. It's on page 12. Sunday Mercury enters Gemini and your mind could be very busy for the next few weeks. A hunger for learning, studying, reporting out what you've disseminated will all be available. You may notice you speak faster or perhaps your mouth can't keep up with your brain and you trip over words. Be certain your intelligence is amplified now, use the transit wisely by starting a new course, reading an important book, or writing your first screenplay.

GIFT & SHADOW THIS WEEK: *Money and abundance are the issues we must work through this week. Fear and worry about resources or having "enough" can be the source of our compromising ourselves this week. We are designed to have everything we desire, which demands that we trust in the abundant nature of the Universe and then align ourselves emotionally with being worthy of receiving. This week's high side is bounteousness, and in the low, we have compromised what we love and want, for we feel we have no choice but to settle.*

MONDAY, MAY 26 – SUNDAY, JUNE 1	MOONS: TAURUS, GEMINI, CANCER

With all of the activity over the past seven days it's nice that this week you can ruminate on the moon work. A New Moon in Gemini is your opportunity to socialize, share, learn, ask, and ask again what the world needs of you. The New Moon article is one of the holistic resources available monthly. Find it on page 83. After the lunation you can simply notice what Gemini then Cancer energies do to you personally. Continue your notetaking because you are building a reference book for later use. You are amplifying your astrological knowledge. Don't neglect your monthly review Little Pretzel. What changed for you in May? How will you adjust for summer? Remember, a dream without a plan is just a wish.

GIFT & SHADOW THIS WEEK: *Patience is a virtue, right? With Earth transiting through Gate 34-Power this week, we are tempted to jump and leap into and out of things without waiting, which can become problematic. This is a high-energy week, but we can discover once it's over that we have over-committed ourselves to the wrong things. The Sun at Gate 20-Patience asks you to wait long enough to know what is right for you and then choose your next steps. Otherwise, you may find that when what you truly desire comes along, you don't have the time or space to participate. PS: if you don't have that "knowing" of what is correct, then it's best to wait.*

May Moon Work

MAY 12, 12:56 PM FULL MOON AT 22° SCORPIO	○ **THE MYSTERIES OF MONEY**

Don't keep secrets! If you're feeling especially interested in money today it's really no surprise. The mysterious sign of Scorpio is being triggered by the sun and Uranus both in Taurus. Sudden insights about the budget might be kept close to the vest and you have permission to do so if you need to. The moon is in a harmonious aspect with Saturn working at adding discipline to your visualizations and creativity. What fabulous partners they make to assist you in paying attention to the right timing for these activities. The issue could be that there are ideas dropping in that need addressing and maybe you're caught up daydreaming or being mysterious.

Today we have the moon nudging Neptune asking you to apply intuition more often inside of your leadership roles. If you're feeling this closely don't be alarmed, simply make note of the intuitive hits and act on them accordingly and always at the right time.

Your thoughts are naturally slower and more practical right now and under this moon could bring up an interest in creating change that would affect your leadership style. Let your passion lead!

AFFIRMATION: *"I am easily receiving insights and information that benefit me now."*

MOON WORK:

- Capture ideas as they arise by using your Notes app on your phone or a journal by your bedside. Spend time figuring out what might be the right time to act on these ideas.
- Scorpio is interested in transformation. What topics are you intuitively drawn to? Make a plan to start looking into them.
- Joint finances are the topic of Scorpio. Be sure to look at debt and consider where you could reduce or eliminate it; this is good use of Full Moon energy!

_____

_____

_____

_____

_____

_____

_____

_____

_____

_____

✼ Get your book bonus offers: www.choosebigchange.com/pages/bonus25 ✼

MAY 26, 11:02 PM
NEW MOON AT 6° GEMINI

CURIOUS ABOUT LEADING

This fire-filled moon is sure to activate a curious and engaged mind. The sun and moon and Mercury in Gemini, currently conjunct one another, are also conjunct Uranus generating sudden insights about the economy or your own personal funds. Revelations could be quite shocking. At the very least, you could find yourself asking questions about your budget or how your self-talk is affecting your livelihood. Neptune and Pluto have large parts to play during the New Moon. Neptune is encouraging the sun, moon, and Mercury toward a loving style of leadership to benefit and Pluto is telling them "It's for the future good of the group."

With Saturn just entering the early degrees of Aries and playing kindly with Mercury, ideas of harnessing your leadership skills are top of mind, too.

The real tensions of the day are created by Jupiter who is wearing the color-blocked shirt of Gemini. He's "poking the bears" of Saturn in Aries, Neptune in Aries, and the north node in Pisces. What Jupiter wants is to magnify your curiosity for your own edification and get you to stand tall, be brave, and be seen as a leader who isn't afraid of their own individuality.

Your passion could be high, direct it creatively to develop goals for the next thirty days that encourage soul-fueled actions.

AFFIRMATION: *"I am asking good questions and listening for great answers as I lead the charge."*

MOON WORK:

- Spend time thinking about a leader you respect. List the qualities of that person and then pick two skills or attributes to develop in that vein.
- Meditate on the topic of leadership while asking the question, "What do I need to know about myself and leadership now?"
- Gemini are social. Be sure to gather with friends to discuss these topics.

_____

_____

_____

_____

_____

_____

_____

_____

_____

_____

♡ Fun, fresh, transformational products + services: https://choosebigchange.com ♡

Numerology

Numerologically this is a five month in a nine year.
May = 5 and 2025 = 9; 5 + 9 = 14; 1 + 4 = 5

Five is the number of movement and adventure. Don't be surprised if this month involves some twists and turns. Apply the wisdom of past mis-adventures so that you don't repeat mistakes.

Gemstones & Oils

GEMSTONES

Moldavite This piece connects you directly to divine source, is a potent heart healer, helps manifest your best, rapid transformation, and allows dreams to become reality.

Dendritic Agate Welcomes abundance, inner peace, personal growth, open perspective, calms the nervous system, releases arrogance, and nudges one to have the discipline to move forward.

OILS

Clary Sage *Salvia sclarea*
Intuitive, clarity, euphoric, inspiring
Blends well w/ Grapefruit, Lavender, Neroli, Frankincense

Clary sage aids in relaxation and stimulation at the same time, making it wonderful for expanding our dreams. Diffusing at bedtime can help you shut down the burdensome thoughts that keep us held back all while activating our wildest dreams with clarity from our third eye.

Nutmeg *Myristica fragrans*
Mystical, dream enhancing, warming
Blends well w/ Grapefruit, Bay Laurel, Geranium, Sandalwood

Nutmeg packs a punch for such a sweet smelling aroma. It's as though she lures you in with her soft compassion and trustful hand to lull you to dream land, where she warms and inspires you with mystical visions through the nite. Her warmth removes your worries in the moment and her spiciness says "dare to dream, expand your horizons."

_____

_____

_____

_____

_____

Rhythms, Routines & Rituals

The impossible dream requires a combination of bold vision, persistence, and self-belief. Play with these routines to leverage this month's energies to achieve your wild audacious dreams (or even little dreams).

- **Vision Board Creation:** Create a vision board with images and words that represent your impossible dream. Keep it visible so it's top of mind. I snap a photo and use mine as my screensaver.

- **Morning Visualization:** Practice visualizing when you wake. Vividly imagine achieving your dream. Include specific details and emotions associated with your goal, involving all of your senses.

- **Goal Setting and Planning:** Break down your impossible dream into smaller, actionable goals. Develop a strategic plan with realistic timelines and milestones to track your progress. Baby steps, baby!

- **Daily Affirmations:** Incorporate daily affirmations that reinforce your belief in achieving the impossible. For example:

  - "I am capable of achieving the impossible, and I trust in my ability to make my dreams a reality."

  - "I attract positive opportunities and align with the energy needed to manifest my impossible dream."

We often get it backwards, thinking that HAVING something will enable us to BE who we want. Try reverse engineering: Be, Do, Have. Be what you desire first, then do what needs to be done to get you there, then you will call in that impossible dream. For other ways to crush your goals grab my bonus material.

_____

_____

_____

_____

_____

_____

_____

_____

_____

GET YOUR FREE BONUS CONTENT AT:
WWW.CHOOSEBIGCHANGE.COM/PAGES/BONUS25

Scan here

♡ Fun, fresh, transformational products + services: https://choosebigchange.com ♡

Wisdom Diaries

My Dearest Great-Grandmother,

Even though you're no longer with us, I still feel your presence and wisdom guiding me through life. I've been thinking a lot about how to keep a positive outlook and imagine a better future, and I can't help but wish I could ask for your advice.

You were always so good at seeing the bright side of things, even when times were tough. Your imagination seemed limitless, and you never stopped believing in the good things yet to come. I remember how you taught our family to trust in God's plan, and breathe deeply when we were feeling off-kilter.

I'm reaching out to you now, hoping you can share some of that wisdom with me. How can I tap into my own imagination to envision a world full of love, peace, and abundance? And how can I use that vision to make positive changes in my life and the lives of others?

You faced your fair share of challenges, but you never lost hope. I admire that about you, and I want to learn how to cultivate that same sense of optimism and possibility.

Even though you're not here in person, I know your spirit lives on, and your wisdom continues to guide me. Thank you for being a source of light and inspiration in my life, now and always.

> With love,
> Your Great-Grandchild

My Dearest Grandchild,

Your heartfelt letter touched my spirit deeply, and I am honored that you seek my guidance even beyond the veil. Though my physical presence may have crossed into the light, my love for you remains eternal, and I am always here to offer my wisdom and support.

I am immensely proud of the thoughtful, compassionate person you have become. Your desire to harness the power of imagination and positivity to create a brighter future is a testament to your beautiful soul and the values instilled in you.

Remember, my dear, that imagination knows no bounds. Allow your mind to wander freely, envisioning a world filled with love, joy, and endless possibilities. Hold onto those visions with unwavering faith, for they have the power to manifest into reality through your actions and intentions. It is in this way we are able to anchor the light of potential into the energetic matrix, and call in a higher timeline for ourselves and for all.

But also, be gentle with yourself. Life is a journey filled with twists and turns, and it's okay to stumble along the way. Embrace each challenge as an opportunity for growth, knowing that every setback brings you closer to your dreams.

Continue to walk your path with courage, kindness, and an open heart. And know that wherever your journey takes you, my love and support will be with you every step of the way.

> With all my love and blessings,
> Your Great-Grandmother

Month End Review

What was new, good, and different about this month?

_____

_____

_____

_____

_____

_____

_____

_____

_____

_____

_____

_____

_____

_____

_____

_____

_____

_____

_____

_____

_____

_____

_____

Energy Almanac 2025 Edition

June

EXPANSIVE EMOTIONAL OUTPUT

JUNE 2-8
DO some work concerning self-worth.
DO NOT speak carelessly, your words
are creative.

JUNE 9-15
DO work that aligns with your passion.
DO NOT "do" for the sake of "doing."

JUNE 16-22
DO partake in a Solstice event.
DO NOT share unless the audience is right.

JUNE 23-29
DO pause for added clarity.
DO NOT avoid a month-end review.

WHAT AM I READY TO DO OR BE THAT WOULD ACTIVATE MY LIFE IN A GENERATIVE WAY?

JUNE 11, 3:44 AM
FULL MOON AT 20° SAGITTARIUS
IMAGINING NEW ADVENTURES

JUNE 25, 6:31 AM
NEW MOON AT 4° CANCER
EXPANSIVE ANCESTRAL WISDOM

Energy Almanac 2025 EDITION

♡ Love the Energy Almanac? Tag us on social media: @TheEnergyAlmanac ♡

Month At-A-Glance

◇◆◇

Write in the dates of this month before taking a few minutes to make notes of specific astrological time periods as they intersect with your own life happenings. You may even choose to highlight those time periods in green and red to remind yourself of easy and difficult days.

MONDAY	TUESDAY	WEDNESDAY	THURSDAY	FRIDAY	SATURDAY	SUNDAY

 Notes

June

You are half way through the year, friend. With the warmth of June's sun in the northern hemisphere come some interesting planetary challenges. Jupiter is having conversations with Uranus, Saturn and Neptune this month. Uranus is working with economics while Saturn and Neptune are both in the early degrees of Aries autonomous energy. You have leadership and actions that are flavored with expansive emotional output and intuitive information. Let's all agree to move carefully through the month; don't let the boldness or aggression of Aries take the lead. Stay in your heart. Make plans for a summer solstice gathering. The Full Moon in Sagittarius is a chance to look at your own routine beliefs and how you truth tell while the New Moon in Cancer is an opportunity for new intentions around homelife and emotional output. Don't forget on June 20 to stand under the expansive universe and give thanks for everything you've experienced so far this year.

TRANSITS

6/6	**Venus enters Taurus**
6/8	**Mercury enters Cancer**
6/9	**Jupiter enters Cancer**
6/11	**Full Moon at 20° Sagittarius,** read moon article
6/17	**Mars enters Virgo**
6/18	**International Picnic Day**
6/19	**Yod: Mars, Pluto, Saturn, Neptune**
6/19	**Yod: Pluto, Jupiter, Mars**
6/20	**Sun enters Cancer, Happy Birthday, Cancerians!**
6/20	**Summer Solstice**
6/22	**Yod: Pluto, Sun, Jupiter, Mars**
6/25	**New Moon at 4° Cancer,** read moon article
6/26	**Mercury enters Leo**

RESOURCES

Numerology: 6 month in a 9 year

Gemstones: Blue Apatite, Rainbow Moonstone

Oils: Bergamot, Frankincense

Rituals: Emotional Excavation

Wisdom Diaries: Emotional Maturity & Evolution

ORACLE PLAY

"What do I need to know about the month ahead?"

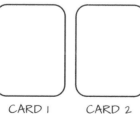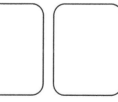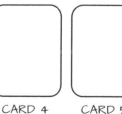

CARD 1   CARD 2   CARD 3   CARD 4   CARD 5

_____

_____

_____

_____

_____

♡ Fun, fresh, transformational products + services: https://choosebigchange.com ♡

JUNE PREDICTIONS

MONDAY, JUNE 2 – SUNDAY, JUNE 8	**MOONS:** LEO, VIRGO, LIBRA

The month is open and the week begins with playful energy before becoming more practical mid-week. Use the playful energy to work with your inner child by grabbing a donut. Monday is National Donut day in America. On Friday Venus, planet of relations, will enter Taurus a place where she is mightily comfortable. Here we find ourselves actively addressing our resources such as money and tangibles as well as our personal self-worth. This is a period of figuring out if you really believe you deserve more. That kind of work can reap big rewards. Celebrate yourself with a beautiful bouquet of flowers, something every Taurean would appreciate. Sunday Mercury will slip into the bunny slippers and fluffy pink housecoat of Cancer. Communication will soften, words will nurture, and chances are good that you'll find yourself ruminating on things at home. Emotional language will turn up and logic turns down. Take a selfie of you and your flower bouquet or your home and tag us in your social post. We are @TheEnergyAlmanac.

GIFT & SHADOW THIS WEEK: *With the Sun in Gate 35-Experience and the Earth in Gate 5-Rhythm, we face opposing forces this week. One force that wants adventure and experiences and another that feels like "been there, done that," and there's nothing new for me to learn. The first leads us to new experiences we can share with others. It's the story of triumph and exploration. The second one makes us feel jaded, restless, and bored with life, leading us to settle for the status quo. Which will you choose? The Gate 35 is on the Throat Center (communication & manifestation) and the Gate 5 is on the Sacral Center. This pairing brings our voice together with our actions—be careful with language this week as it holds creative power.*

_____
_____
_____
_____
_____
_____
_____
_____

FEELING **HAPPY?** CHECK THIS OUT!

WWW.CHOOSEBIGCHANGE.COM/PRODUCTS/HAPPY-YOUR-FAVORITE-COMFY-SWEATSHIRT

MONDAY, JUNE 9 – SUNDAY, JUNE 15

MOONS: SCORPIO, SAGITTARIUS, CAPRICORN

Another important societal transit is upon us this week and it starts on Monday afternoon when the planet of expansion—Jupiter—moves into Cancer. Without being redundant, we highly recommend a new notebook just for this transit. Jupiter, bringer of luck, opportunity, and expansion is slipping into the housecoat of Cancer. Slippers on, tissue nearby, expect your intuition and emotion to be amplified. Home Life has never been so wonderful as when Jupiter is cocooning in Cancer. Over time this transit will be felt across the globe and we are enjoying imagining a massive return to home life and use of ancestral wisdom. Imagine the gathering of families around the dining room table. See the nurturing of children and of each other all while our intuitions are alight with information. Meditate on the many potentials and write down what your intuition tells you. Wednesday is a Full Moon in Sagittarius and you'll feel a sense of adventure and fun and high hopes for your future. Read and apply the information in our moon article on page 96. Sunday the two societal planets, Jupiter and Saturn, will square off. Jupiter in the early degrees of Cancer is in one corner and Saturn in Aries stands in the opposite corner. Both want what they want and in the stand off action will be triggered. Stay home and take care of each other or stand up and lead? There is room for both.

GIFT & SHADOW THIS WEEK: *What if I told you that prosperity was a natural effect of you aligning with your passion? That is precisely what this week brings us. The potential for monetary gain isn't always linked to what we do. It is more appropriately linked to who we are in our authentic expression. This week, with the Sun in Gate 45, a potent money Gate, avoid the pressure of doing something to make money, as it is not fulfilling (unless making money is your passion). Follow your passions to express yourself in fulfilling and authentic ways. Then money and abundance will flow to you effortlessly and naturally. After all, the Earth in Gate 26-Integrity clarifies that doing otherwise would not support that financial flow!*

_____

_____

_____

_____

_____

_____

_____

_____

_____

♡ Fun, fresh, transformational products + services: https://choosebigchange.com ♡

MONDAY, JUNE 16 — SUNDAY, JUNE 22

MOONS: AQUARIUS, PISCES, ARIES, TAURUS

Oh boy. This week is another one to watch. Tuesday Mars moves into Virgo. Imagine a star athlete wearing a lab coat. The practical action and a hyper-analytical service oriented mind will come into play and will move through you. Perhaps you'll take action toward holistic health modalities, it's a Mars in Virgo possibility. Wednesday, also International Picnic Day, Jupiter in Cancer squares Neptune in Aries. Here, as you nibble sandwiches or salad, you have to look at high emotions and spiritual leadership. Maybe your intuition is saying one thing and your boldness is bringing you in the opposite direction. Maybe the two ideas coalesce into a benevolent leadership move? June 19 is a Thursday for the books when two different yods form. Yods are called "the finger of God" and are astrological aspects that create events that can be important. It's best we wait and see what shakes out, but know that there is plenty going on with the planets!

The sun enters Cancer and we can celebrate our emotional, nurturing Cancer friends and family members as you yourself notice more intuitive hits over the next four weeks. If that wasn't enough, the summer solstice is pleasantly placed on Saturday. Seek out a ritual that can ground in the potent message of the longest day of the year. On Sunday the third yod of the week employs Pluto, Sun, Jupiter and Mars. With more prospective events on the table, this week is sure to leave its mark on the rest of 2025.

The best resource for a seven day run of planetary movement is writing. Make notes of what is going on in the greater landscape as well as what is happening to yourself internally and close to home. There is much wisdom to be gained by recognizing and reflecting on patterns in your life. Trust me when I say you'll refer back to this week at another date.

GIFT & SHADOW THIS WEEK: *The Sun is in Gate 12-Caution, in the Throat Center, and Earth is in Gate 11-Ideas, in the Ajna this week. The gift of Gate 12 is the ability to speak at the right time in a way that uplifts and elevates others. The caution here is that the right timing is always linked to mood. Being in the mood equals beautiful words; not being in the mood means stumbling, trying to get the right words, and all the words need to be clearer. This can be especially trying with the Earth in Gate 11 because we are filled with wonderful ideas that we want to share with others or that we want to take action on ourselves. Be cautious about sharing. Be sure you address the right audience at the right time to be seen, heard, valued, and recognized!*

MONDAY, JUNE 23 – SUNDAY, JUNE 29

MOONS: TAURUS, GEMINI, CANCER

The end of June wraps up with a beautiful New Moon in Cancer offering you the opportunity to make promises to yourself about how you will use your intuition and come into alignment with your own nurturing capacity. Read more about this lunation in the holistic resources for this month on page 97. Thursday Mercury, the cosmic communicator, will move into the sign of Leo and a sudden vitality flavors your language. Creative expression is on high and along with it a refined way of speaking. Perhaps thou might employ a more royal tone for the next many weeks? Thou may find themselves quite entertaining as well. Enjoy the transit and pay attention to see if you find yourself generally more animated.

GIFT & SHADOW THIS WEEK: *The Sun is in Gate 52-Stillness this week, which concerns our ability to know what to focus our time and attention on. In the shadow, this can feel like ADHD, when we have so much to do that we end up zipping from one thing to another without ever finishing. Sometimes, it is stillness that is called for. A pause before taking action to gain clarity over what the step is. This week, learn that relaxation is a stress reliever and taking on too much or feeling pushed to do it all, creates stress. After all, with the Earth in Gate 58-Joy, we are meant to remember that happiness and bliss are more accessible to experience when we are present and still.*

_____

_____

_____

_____

_____

_____

_____

_____

_____

_____

_____

ENERGY ALMANAC CHALLENGE: How will you use your intuition to align with your nurturing capacity? Share your intentions via a post on FB or IG. Tag us with @theenergyalmanac so we can cheer you on.

♡ Fun, fresh, transformational products + services: https://choosebigchange.com ♡

June Moon Work

JUNE 11, 3:44 AM	◯ IMAGINING NEW ADVENTURES
FULL MOON AT 20° SAGITTARIUS	

The ever optimistic and adventuresome Sagittarius moon is as bright as its Sagittarian outlook and brings with it a boatload of planetary action. The moon is being aspected by Mars, the north node and Chiron. Creative expression is elevated (Mars) but there is tension about your individuality. Perhaps it's a lack of confidence playing out? Stand tall and let go of any fear of being seen being fully you. Mercury, your lower mind, is also busy today. It is playing well with Venus and Jupiter. These two planets are urging an interest in pimping out your nest. Jupiter and Mars are encouraging creativity at home, too. Shopping anyone? If you do venture out, remember to be disciplined and thoughtful in your spending. Saturn is encouraging you to remember you are a leader with strong intuition. Employ it as you will!

At a higher, more soulful level, Neptune and Pluto are having a chat. Heart-centered leadership as it relates to humanitarianism, the digital landscape, and innovation are encouraged. With the moon rightly activated with Sagittarian spunk you may develop some big ideas worth exploring.

AFFIRMATION: *"I am expecting great things, my big ideas are beautiful."*

MOON WORK:

- Direct some energy toward releasing old beliefs that only keep you playing small, use emotional freedom technique for deep healing.
- Tweak your home environment creatively. Add style and flare (Mars in Leo) using what you already have at home by moving things around.
- Rate your confidence. Have you been willing to be courageous and adventure outside of your comfort zone? Brain dump all the ideas you have for new ways to grow your confidence.

_____
_____
_____
_____
_____
_____
_____
_____
_____
_____

JUNE 25, 6:31 AM
NEW MOON AT 4° CANCER

 EXPANSIVE ANCESTRAL WISDOM

The two luminaries of note, Sun and Moon, are sure to be triggered. There are multiple planets teasing, poking, and prodding you and emotional output could be extremely high in particular due to Jupiter's magnification of your feelings. Lean toward diplomacy and practicality as you work your way through this new moon. Mars is nearby (sextile) the sun and moon, offering some muscle that can support the variety of thoughts that may flow through you at this time.

If tensions arise it could be caused by boldness ill-timed or being overly aggressive in nature. Here is your second cry for applying diplomacy before reacting.

Uranus is in his final degree of Taurus dropping final thought about resources both personally and on the greater world landscape. He's teasing Mars in the sign of Virgo suggesting you employ your intelligence to fiscal matters. At the same time Pluto is forcing thoughts of group energy and innovation. It is easy to see that your head and your heart may be at odds. Uranus is playing with both Saturn and Neptune. Where Uranus arrives, expect revelation, perhaps shocking insights worth further thought.

Also in the cosmos tonight is Jupiter, the great cheerleader, encouraging use of your intuition and urging you to use your ancestral wisdom within your compassionate leadership style.

AFFIRMATION: *"I am a strong, calm, and intuitive leader always doing the best I can with what I have."*

MOON WORK:

* Capture new ideas on paper. Uranus is surely going to send you some information, it's best you write it down.
* Ancestral wisdom is passed down through the generations. List your grandparents as far back as you can, and then write what you know about their skills, talents, and wisdom.
* Meditate on the topic of family leadership to discover more about who you can be.

_____

_____

_____

_____

_____

_____

_____

_____

_____

_____

♡ Fun, fresh, transformational products + services: https://choosebigchange.com ♡

Numerology

Numerologically this is a six month in a nine year.
June = 6 and 2025 = 9; 6 + 9 = 15; 1 + 5 = 6

Six is the number of love and nurturing. This soft energy applied with the knowledge of nine can add a nice flavor of harmony to the opening of the next season. Domestic happiness is here and you can feel fully secure.

Gemstones & Oils

GEMSTONES

Blue Apatite Enhances clarity and clairvoyance, speaks ideas into reality, expands intellect, clears and cleanses negative emotions—helps one to give and receive with more ease.

Rainbow Moonstone Heightens awareness and intuition, welcomes new beginnings and positive emotions, enhances confidence and feelings, embodies the energies of summer solstice and the moon. This is a great buffer to have during disagreements and misunderstandings.

OILS

Bergamot *Citrus bergamia*
Letting go, uplifting, trauma healing
Blends well w/ Chamomile, Lavender, Frankincense, Basil, Cedarwood

Bergamot is the perfect oil to keep you light yet expansive while processing deep emotional aspects such as self worth, generational karma and childhood trauma. It keeps your emotions open and moving forward giving an alternative, and perhaps new, perspective of the past.

Frankincense *Boswellia carterii*
Spiritual liberation, protection, balancing
Blends well w/ Rose, Citrus, Jasmine, Patchouli, Cedarwood, Cypress

Frankincense is the oil of spirituality. It helps you to stay connected to your breath, it slows you down, allowing you to meditate, pray and focus, in order to see messages more clearly. It has been used for centuries in spiritual practices encouraging connection with our ancestors. Frankincense is beneficial for cutting ties or blocks from the past for purposes of personal growth.

_____

_____

_____

_____

_____

Rhythms, Routines & Rituals

The June energy prompts us to do some emotional excavation. Journaling is your secret weapon to decode the emotional rollercoaster we call life. It's not just a diary; it's your backstage pass to self-discovery. Let's give it a try, shall we?

- How are you feeling right now, and can you describe that emotion in more detail?
- What events or situations have triggered these emotions?
- Can you recall a specific moment or memory when you felt a similar emotion in the past?
- What do these emotions tell you about your current needs, desires, or values?
- In what ways do you express or cope with these emotions?
- Is there a physical sensation associated with these emotions? How does it manifest in your body?
- Are there any underlying beliefs or assumptions influencing how you interpret and respond to these emotions?
- What might help you feel more supported or understood at this moment?
- If you could choose an image, color or metaphor to represent your emotions, what would it be, and why?
- What strengths or resources do you possess that could support you in navigating and understanding these emotions?

Getting introspective can help you recalibrate and prepare you to move forward into the secosnd half of the year, and a new season. Want to dig deeper? Be sure to grab my bonus material.

_____

_____

_____

_____

_____

_____

_____

GET YOUR FREE BONUS CONTENT AT:
WWW.CHOOSEBIGCHANGE.COM/PAGES/BONUS25

Scan here

♡ Fun, fresh, transformational products + services: https://choosebigchange.com ♡

Dear Inner Being,

As I navigate the complexities of emotional maturity and evolution, I often find myself grappling with the fear of vulnerability. Opening my heart fully feels like standing on the edge of a cliff, unsure of whether I'll fly or fall. But I know deep down that true growth lies in embracing vulnerability, in allowing myself to feel deeply and authentically, even when it's uncomfortable.

Loving myself is another journey I'm embarking on, one that requires patience, compassion, and a willingness to embrace my flaws and imperfections. It's easy to be my own harshest critic, but I'm learning to silence that inner voice of doubt and replace it with one of kindness and acceptance. I'm learning to treat myself with the same love and care that I so readily give to others, recognizing that I am worthy of love and belonging just as I am.

And then there's holding spacious love for others, a concept that both inspires and challenges me. It's about extending grace, understanding, and empathy to those around me, even when my ego might feel they do not deserve it. It's about seeing the humanity in others, even when they may be difficult or hurtful. It's about recognizing that we are all flawed and imperfect beings, doing the best we can with what we have and despite all that, we are better working together.

Inner Being, I come to you with an open heart and a humble spirit, seeking your guidance on this journey of emotional expansiveness, self-love, and holding spacious love for others. Help me to cultivate the courage to be vulnerable, the compassion to love myself fiercely, and the wisdom to extend grace to those around me. With your light as my guide, I know that I can navigate these waters with grace and humility. Thank you for being my constant companion on this journey called life.

With love and gratitude,
Me

My Dear You!

Your sentiments resonate deeply within me, and fill our being with a sense of warmth and gratitude. It's an honor to be entrusted with your innermost thoughts and feelings, and I want you to know that I am here for you every step of the way.

As you embark on the journey of emotional expansiveness, self-love, and holding space for others, I want to remind you that you are already equipped with everything you need to succeed. Within you lies an infinite well of courage, compassion, and wisdom waiting to be tapped into.

Embracing vulnerability can be scary, but it is also incredibly liberating. It is through vulnerability that we find connection, authenticity, and true intimacy with ourselves and others. Allow yourself to lean into vulnerability with an open heart, knowing that it is a sign of strength, not weakness.

Loving yourself is a journey of self-discovery and self-acceptance. It's about embracing all aspects of yourself—the light and the shadow, the strengths and the vulnerabilities. Be gentle with yourself, my dear, and remember that you are worthy of love and belonging simply because you exist.

And when it comes to holding spacious love for others, let compassion be your guiding light. Seek to understand rather than to judge, to empathize rather than to criticize. Remember that we are all on our own unique journey, navigating life as best we can. Extend grace generously, both to others and to yourself.

Know that you are never alone on this journey. I am here, always, whispering words of encouragement, guiding you towards greater expansiveness, deeper self-love, and more compassion for others. Trust in yourself, trust in the process, and trust in the power of love to transform and heal.

With unwavering love and support,
Your Inner Being

Month End Review

❖◇❖

What was new, good, and different about this month?

♡ Fun, fresh, transformational products + services: https://choosebigchange.com ♡

July

SOCIALLY STUNNING

JUNE 30–JULY 6

DO plan a weekend adventure.
DO NOT fall into a lack mentality.

JULY 7–13

DO a thorough re-evaluation.
DO NOT forget to tweak your goals.

JULY 14–20

DO plan a weekend gathering.
DO NOT be impatient with others.

JULY 21–27

DO choose peace over drama.
DO NOT avoid a month-end review.

WHAT BENEFIT CAN IT BE TO ASK QUESTIONS SOCIALLY?

JULY 10, 4:37 PM

FULL MOON AT 18° CAPRICORN
THE BUSINESS OF INTUITIVE LEADERSHIP

JULY 24, 3:11 PM

NEW MOON AT 2° LEO
ROYAL AND LOYAL

Energy Almanac 2025 EDITION

Month At-A-Glance

◇ ◇ ◇

Write in the dates of this month before taking a few minutes to make notes of specific astrological time periods as they intersect with your own life happenings. You may even choose to highlight those time periods in green and red to remind yourself of easy and difficult days.

MONDAY	TUESDAY	WEDNESDAY	THURSDAY	FRIDAY	SATURDAY	SUNDAY

Notes

July

July has some planetary moves that we can collectively learn from. With the large generational planet Uranus who wants to bring revelation, shifting into the student's color-blocked button down shirt of Gemini, education will become part of the subconscious mind. Uranus will tour Gemini for the next seven years giving you plenty of time to participate in the future of education and the changing of social networks. Personal planet Venus is also going to be wearing Gemini's pocket-protected shirt this month which will add a social vivaciousness to the days ahead. It's good timing for you to plan gatherings and have important conversations. Gemini is not just social, it's curious, too. Expect to ask a lot of questions. Mid-month Mercury will retrograde in the playful sign of Leo and passion may be quieted for a short while as you review creative expression. The Full Moon in Capricorn will have a serious edge, but the New Moon in Leo is a chance to play. Ask good questions in July and expect good answers.

TRANSITS

7/4	**Venus enters Gemini**
7/4	**Neptune Retrograde in Aries**
7/7	**Uranus enters Gemini**
7/7	**World Chocolate Day**
7/10	**Full Moon at 18° Capricorn,** read moon article
7/13	**Saturn Retrograde in Aries**
7/18	**Mercury Retrograde in Leo**
7/22	**Sun enters Leo, Happy Birthday, Leo!**
7/24	**New Moon at 2° Leo,** read moon article
7/30	**Venus enters Cancer**

RESOURCES

Numerology: 7 month in a 9 year

Gemstones: Aventurine, Opal

Oils: Neroli, Ginger

Rituals: Daily Confidence Boost, Get Curious And Ask Questions, Practice Active Listening Habits, Bring Your 'A' Game

Wisdom Diaries: Tapping Into Our Collective Wisdom

ORACLE PLAY

"What do I need to know about the month ahead?"

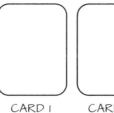   

CARD 1   CARD 2   CARD 3   CARD 4   CARD 5

_____

_____

_____

_____

Energy Almanac 2025 Edition

♡ Fun, fresh, transformational products + services: https://choosebigchange.com ♡

JULY PREDICTIONS

MONDAY, JUNE 30 – SUNDAY, JULY 6	MOONS: LEO, VIRGO, LIBRA, SAGITTARIUS

Little Pretzel, rest easy. June ends and your only real task is to use your analytical Virgo mind to review and reflect on the month and then set goals while keeping in mind that at least in the United States, it's summer. Don't overbook yourself so that you miss out on the sunshine. Friday is the only real transit of the week to mention. Venus, the cosmic Marilyn Monroe, ruler of love and money, will pull on the color-blocked button down shirt of "student" Gemini making one extremely curious inside of relationships and quite social, too. This transit could find you showing the more childish side of yourself. Keep that in mind as you bump into trouble over the month of July. This weekend looks like a good one for adventure. Perhaps plan a hike or go zip lining. Let us know what you choose. Tag us in your social media @TheEnergyAlmanac.

GIFT & SHADOW THIS WEEK: *The Sun is at Gate 39-Provocation, and the Earth at Gate 38-Struggle this week, setting us up for possible fireworks of the emotional kind. The shadows in this Gate are huge. There is the potential for eating disorders, hoarding behaviors, and shopping as "retail therapy" here, to name a few. A subtle feeling of "not enoughness" and lack of faith can cause us to lapse into a lack mentality. The gift here is that provocation pushes us toward having more faith and trust in a higher power and allowing abundance to flow freely. What can I say about the Earth at the Gate of Struggle? Life here is grounded in struggle, it is an evolutionary principle. But, we do not need to allow struggle to devolve into suffering. It's a choice. Make a wise one!*

MONDAY, JULY 7 – SUNDAY, JULY 13	MOONS: SAGITTARIUS, CAPRICORN, AQUARIUS

Monday is stellar! It's no cosmic joke that this week begins with World Chocolate day and in the early morning you are awakened to a universal shift that will rock your world for the next seven years. Uranus, the planet of revelation, will enter Gemini. With Uranus words like futuristic, innovative, insightful, sudden, revelatory, digital all come into play. With Gemini, close to home words are studying, learning, duality, social, witty but in the mundane world we are talking about education. Uranus has arrived to start the journey of changing education. Watch how the future of our learning institutions change. Expect flashes of insight as to what it can look like to learn with AI or change how public schools teach. What if students learn completely unique topics outside of math, science, and reading? This incredible transit is sure to serve the greater good. How will you participate? Make a list of things you appreciate about the current system, and a second list about what you'd change. Start there and keep the list in a place where you can later check off what shifted under the Uranus in Gemini transit. On page 12 of this Almanac you can reference the "Important Planetary Moves" article for more information.

Thursday is the Full Moon in Capricorn which will give a serious flavor to releasing what isn't foundational to your goals. Read the details in our moon article for this month.

GIFT & SHADOW THIS WEEK: *Interestingly, the Sun is in Gate 53-Starting things this week, while the Earth and Full Moon are in Gate 54-Ambition. Usually, we think of the full Moon as a time of release and completion. Still, it also holds the energy of full light, which can help us see where changes can occur. It's a time of potential new beginnings in the middle of a cycle. This is about re-evaluating where you are in your creative cycle, tweaking your goals, and moving forward. It's time to ascend to your super-abundant self!*

MONDAY, JULY 14 – SUNDAY, JULY 20

MOONS: PISCES, ARIES, TAURUS

Summer, summer, summer. This week the cosmos are kept clean and simple with only the moon to wash over you and flavor the next seven days. The week opens with flowing creative, compassionate Pisces energy before shifting to the more bold and action-filled Aries influence. The weekend will bring the perfect state for tending the garden and hosting a small gathering at your nest. Taurus love all things earthy, foody, and money. Our best suggestion: Have all guests bring their favorite salad and associated recipe card for sharing. You can spend your time cutting fresh flowers and writing personalized placards with affirmations on them. Take pictures and tag us in your post.

GIFT & SHADOW THIS WEEK: *Rather than focus on the Sun and Earth for this week's Gift & Shadow, let's look at Uranus, the planet of awakening, shocks, and genius, as he has moved into a new Gate, the Gate 20-Patience, in our Human Design evolution map. His presence in this Gate indicates a shift in the collective consciousness and potential for radical transformation and innovation. We are challenged to express our individuality and authenticity without compromising our integrity or harmony. We are invited to tap into our inner source of power and creativity and to share it with the world at the right time. Patience is required in order to be heard. Be prepared for sudden changes, surprises, and disruptions that test your resilience and flexibility.*

_____

_____

_____

MONDAY, JULY 21 – SUNDAY, JULY 27

MOONS: GEMINI, CANCER, LEO

Last week was astrologically light but these next seven days have some zest. On Tuesday the sun enters Leo, the zodiac's royalty. Notice as you show more strength and zeal for life. Observe how you are more expressive and playful. Leo is a fun sign and extremely childlike. It's a great time to employ your sketchbook. Use crayons this time, or chalk! Draw using your non-dominant hand or using your dominant one, draw yourself as a child. Later in the week on Thursday you can offer up this drawing under the New Moon in Leo when you set your intentions to be more playful for the next 30 days to see how that might bring you more joy. Remember, we are in a season of expansive curiosity. How does it get any better than that? What else is possible? The moon article is a little further along in this month's pages. Don't miss it.

GIFT & SHADOW THIS WEEK: *Transiting Jupiter in Gate 39-Provocation in Human Design tests our emotional resilience and maturity, bringing up challenges, conflicts, and confrontations that trigger our fears, insecurities, and doubts. But we can also be inspired to break free from limiting patterns, beliefs, and situations that keep us stuck or unhappy. Woo Hoo! It is an opportunity to learn how to respond rather than react, choose peace over drama, align with our true self and purpose, and grow, expand, and transform through the power of provocation.*

_____

_____

_____

_____

♡ Fun, fresh, transformational products + services: https://choosebigchange.com ♡

MONDAY, JULY 28 – SUNDAY, AUGUST 3

MOONS: VIRGO, LIBRA, SCORPIO

The last week of July begins with the practical, no-nonsense energy of Virgo, a great way to open the week if you're prepping the kids to go back to school and ordering supplies for them. As the month winds down on the 30th Venus will slide into Cancer for a short stay. Here you get the experience of a deep love for all things family. You may be especially sensitive at this time, and that's okay. Applied knowledge is power. Expecting you could be more tender than normal means you can respond carefully rather than being reactive.

Little Pretzel, it's the end of another month and we are well past the half-way point of the year. A good review is in order. Are you satisfied with how the year is unfolding? What can you do to be more in flow? What are you succeeding at? Ponder these questions in the warm sun, sip lemonade, and use your journal. There's more than enough time to course correct and end the year on a high note.

GIFT & SHADOW THIS WEEK: *The transiting Sun at Gate 31-Democracy concerns the collective leadership potential of humanity. Democracy in Human Design means anyone can express their opinions and visions and potentially influence others to follow them. However, democracy also requires that the leaders are recognized and supported by the people they lead and act with integrity and responsibility. You may be open to new ideas and perspectives now, which can bring an opportunity for positive change and innovation but also a challenge for maintaining stability and harmony. Remember this: the nature of the Throat Center at which Gate 31 sits is sometimes tricky. It works best when we are invited to share our opinions, ideas, and insights. Blurting out comments can create trouble, so hold your counsel and speak when the timing is right.*

_____

_____

_____

_____

_____

_____

_____

_____

_____

✷ Get your book bonus offers: www.choosebigchange.com/pages/bonus25 ✷

July Moon Work

JULY 10, 4:37 PM		THE BUSINESS OF INTUITIVE
FULL MOON AT 18° CAPRICORN	◯	LEADERSHIP

The business of service and leadership and putting a foundation under them is at the heart of this July full moon. Your heart for "doing" is activated and discernment is elevated by the activation of the north node by both the sun and moon. Venus is giving you the urge to be social and she's calling on Pluto to bring together a group. A good topic of conversation could be how to develop strong, soulful, intuitive leaders since there could be some overly brazen leaders on the world scene. With Uranus entering into the first degrees of Gemini there could be some real gems dropped into the conversation concerning education, social media, and even transportation. If the ideas are timed right and delivered well, the greater good could surely benefit.

Let's not forget Jupiter's role on this day. Jupiter is square Saturn. Here expanded intuition is tussling with stern and orderly leadership. It's a good partnership where no matter who wins, we all win. Tapping into your wisdom and applying it in leadership experiences can only benefit everyone. Be sure to not go heavy on one side or the other in order to maintain a balanced approach to the guidance you might be providing at home or at work.

Moon in Capricorn energy is emotionally serious and practical but remember the sun is in Cancer which concerns home life and family. The tug of war is real and there is a time and place for both in your life. Use this lunation to engage in careful consideration about what good leadership looks like in both life areas. Discover what hasn't worked, ditch it, and evolve toward something better.

AFFIRMATION: *"I am serious about my personal development at home and work and it serves the greater good."*

MOON WORK:

- Host an impromptu summer Full Moon party. Invite friends to bring the name of their favorite leader and generate a discussion about the future of leadership.
- Capricorns enjoy the silence and solitude. If this is more your style, then contemplation on the question, "What would help build a solid foundation at home?" could be time well spent.
- Think about home life and decide where or what you could do to bring more order.

_____

_____

_____

_____

_____

_____

_____

♡ Fun, fresh, transformational products + services: https://choosebigchange.com ♡

JULY 24, 3:11 PM
NEW MOON AT 2° LEO

ROYAL AND LOYAL

Under the darkness of the Leo new moon, a real passion for being seen as a royal could develop. Leaders come in all shapes and sizes and have their own unique creative expression and style. So why not you?! It begins with the sun and moon singing in harmony with Saturn and Neptune, both who are working hard to develop good and well-tempered leaders. If there is any strain it is brought forth by Pluto who is encouraging the development of the good of the group. You see, Leo is okay letting it be about "me" while Pluto begs you to transform and make it about the "we." Play with the idea of leading groups from a position of inclusion. Chiron is also activating the sun and moon encouraging more bold individuality so figuring out how to balance the me and the we is a big part of your work.

Futuristic Uranus is dropping some insights tonight. You'll be both surprised and delighted with what your inner senses share with you. With your strong imagination you could intuit some amazing ideas about how to pull your passion and play into a cohesive plan.

The world is changing and you have an important role to play. You are the king or queen of your dominion and your presence will ripple out across your kingdom. Your loyalty toward those you love is important, too. Set intentions for how you can use your own creative spirit within leadership practices. Have fun! Play. The world needs more people having fun.

AFFIRMATION: *"I am bright and capable and passionate about my life."*

MOON WORK:

- You know your creative wheelhouse, use it under this moon. Sing, dance, throw clay, paint, write, whatever it is do it today.
- Journal about the idea of "me v. we" to better understand how you can stand out as a leader but be part of a broader experience.
- Use your non-dominant hand to draw and then color the moon in a landscape. Say or think the affirmation of the month aloud.

_____

_____

_____

_____

_____

_____

_____

_____

_____

_____

_____

Numerology

Numerologically this is a seven month in a nine year.
July = 7 and 2025 = 9; 7 + 9 = 16; 1 + 6 = 7

Seven is a deeply spiritual number. Here you have the chance to employ silence and solitude and expect to receive some inspiration. Together with the ending of cycle energy from the nine perhaps you'll gain perspective about what's next for you.

Gemstones & Oils

GEMSTONES

Aventurine Inspires prosperity, enhances one's luck and ability to see alternative possibilities, brings forward resilience, stabilizes mindset, promotes empathy for oneself and others, and releases old patterns and habits.

Opal Powerful at shifting energetic patterns, aids in decision making, brings intense inner fire to your emotional body, allows insight to others intentions, soothes fear, doubt, irritation, and anger.

OILS

Neroli *Citrus aurantium var. amara*
Euphoric, regal, patience, release
Blends well w/ Rose, Melissa, Patchouli

Neroli knows how to take the stage but not in an over dramatic fashion. She is the princess at the royal gathering known to be sweet, charming, calm, patient, understanding all with a smile and glimmering eye. She encourages patience and the release of that which no longer serves you, making the choice of peace over chaos an easier road to see.

Ginger *Zingiber officinale*
Spontaneous, confident, motivating, stimulating
Blends well w/ Nutmeg, Lemongrass, Orange, Grapefruit, Ylang Ylang

Ginger is warming and stimulating to the circulatory system, encouraging you to be spontaneous, get up and go all with a confident and mentally stimulating drive. Ginger is great for social gatherings when you may feel overworked and need a refreshed, excited mental attitude. It's like putting the fire to your behind, you've never been more driven to move.

_____

_____

_____

_____

♡ Fun, fresh, transformational products + services: https://choosebigchange.com ♡

Rhythms, Routines & Rituals

This month's energy is the perfect time to let your social skills shine. Whether you're in a crowd of strangers or an intimate gathering of friends, this is your chance to get noticed and take charge. Try these strategies to help you stride confidently into the room and interact with ease:

- **Daily Confidence Boost:** Start your day with a confidence-building routine. This could include affirmations, power poses (like the good ol' Wonder Woman pose), or visualizing idea outcomes throughout your day.

- **Get Curious And Ask Questions:** Everyone has a story. Become the most popular person in the room by being interested in others; you may just learn something too!

- **Practice Active Listening Habits:** Develop the habit of active listening. Pay close attention to what others are saying by making eye contact, leaning in and showing genuine interest in their thoughts and feelings.

- **Bring Your 'A' Game:** Put on your favorite outfit, take extra care with make up, wear the good underwear, or don a fun color that makes your eyes pop. Looking good on the outside gives you a boost on the inside as well.

These routines will boost your confidence and help you stand out, but above all, authenticity and being genuine is most important, so just do you. Level up, grab my bonus material.

_____

_____

_____

_____

_____

_____

_____

_____

_____

_____

GET YOUR FREE BONUS CONTENT AT:
WWW.CHOOSEBIGCHANGE.COM/PAGES/BONUS25

Scan here

Wisdom Diaries

Hey Great-Grandpa,

I hope you're doing well up there, watching over us as always. I've been thinking a lot about how we as individuals fit into the bigger picture of humanity's collective consciousness. You always had this knack for understanding people and the world around you, and you taught our family the importance of unity within the community, so I figured you might have some insights to share.

I'm curious about how we can all work together to make things better on a global scale. It feels like we're living in a time of so much division and conflict, and it's easy to feel overwhelmed by it all. But I believe that if we can tap into our collective wisdom and come together with a shared purpose, we can make a real difference.

I know it's not always easy to get along with others, especially when we have different ideas and perspectives. So, I'm wondering how we can navigate those differences and find common ground, even when things get tough. How do we ensure that everyone's voice is heard and respected, even when we don't always agree?

I'm turning to you because I know you have a deep understanding of human nature and a profound respect for the interconnectedness of all living beings. Your wisdom always seemed to transcend time and space, and I'm hoping you can shed some light on this for me.

I'd love to hear your thoughts on group consciousness and collective learning. How can we come together as a global community to create a more harmonious and compassionate world?

> Missing you always,
> Your Great-Grandchild

My Dear,

It warms my heart to receive your letter and to know that you still seek guidance from me, even though I've crossed over to the other side. Rest assured, I am always watching over you and our family, sending my love and blessings your way.

Your questions about group consciousness and collective learning are ones that have intrigued me for quite some time. Humans have a remarkable capacity for connection and collaboration, and it's also true that navigating group dynamics can be tricky, especially when egos and differing opinions come into play.

In my experience, the key to fostering unity within groups lies in cultivating empathy, compassion, and a deep respect for diversity. Each person brings their own unique perspective and life experience to the table, and it's important to honor and value those differences. Instead of seeing them as obstacles, view them as opportunities for growth and understanding.

Listen closely to what others have to say, even if their viewpoints differ from your own. Seek to understand where they're coming from and find common ground whenever possible. Remember that true unity doesn't mean everyone agrees on everything; it means finding ways to work together despite our differences.

As for collective learning, I believe it starts with a willingness to learn from one another and to share our knowledge and insights openly. Be open to new ideas and perspectives, and be generous with your own wisdom and experiences. Together, we can pool our collective knowledge and wisdom to create a brighter, more enlightened future for all.

Above all, remember that you are never alone on this journey. You have a vast network of ancestors, guides, and loved ones who are always here to support and guide you. Trust in yourself, trust in the power of collective wisdom, and trust that together, we can create a world filled with love, compassion, and understanding.

> With all my love,
> Great-Grandpa

Month End Review

◇◇◇

What was new, good, and different about this month?

_____
_____
_____
_____
_____
_____
_____
_____
_____
_____
_____
_____
_____
_____
_____
_____
_____
_____
_____
_____
_____
_____
_____
_____

August

LEADERSHIP AND LEARNING

AUGUST 4-10

DO find the balance between teamwork and "me" work.
DO NOT fail to listen when others speak.

AUGUST 11-17

DO contemplate leadership and learning.
DO NOT shut down to possibilities due to fear.

AUGUST 18-24

DO consider resetting health goals.
DO NOT overcommit.

AUGUST 25-31

DO make decisions from a state of abundance.
DO NOT avoid a month-end review.

WHAT CAN I CREATE AND GENERATE THAT WOULD EXPAND MY LEADERSHIP CAPACITY?

AUGUST 9, 3:55 AM

FULL MOON AT 17° AQUARIUS
PASSIONATE ABOUT CHANGE

AUGUST 23, 2:06 AM

NEW MOON AT 0° VIRGO
SERVICE TO SELF

♡ Love the Energy Almanac? Tag us on social media: @TheEnergyAlmanac ♡

Energy Almanac 2025 Edition

Month At-A-Glance

Write in the dates of this month before taking a few minutes to make notes of specific astrological time periods as they intersect with your own life happenings. You may even choose to highlight those time periods in green and red to remind yourself of easy and difficult days.

MONDAY	TUESDAY	WEDNESDAY	THURSDAY	FRIDAY	SATURDAY	SUNDAY

 Notes

August

As summer heats up, so do the planets. There is plenty of movement overhead some of which involves strong aspects meant as opportunity for growth. The business begins when Mars enters Libra and there is an urge to conjoin. Then Mercury will come out of the retrograde and station direct in the creative and royal sign of Leo bringing with it a royal urge to express yourself. The mid-month sextile between Uranus and Saturn will generate some interesting insights concerning education and leadership and ten days later a "finger of God" presents an interesting moment or two whose outcomes are yet to be determined. We do know that the Sun, Pluto, Saturn, and Neptune are all involved. As the sun moves into Virgo space pragmatism reigns and bringing order to your world feels natural. This could help you navigate a second sextile. This one concerns Uranus and Neptune. It seems leadership and learning are top of mind as we wrap up August. There's heat in the cosmic kitchen. Are you sweating yet?

TRANSITS

8/5	**Grand Trine in air signs...Uranus, Mars, Pluto**
8/6	**Mars enters Libra**
8/7	**Kite: Mars, Pluto, Saturn, Neptune, Uranus**
8/9	**Full Moon at 17° Aquarius,** read moon article
8/11	**Saturn in Aries 12° sextile Uranus in Gemini**
8/11	**Mercury direct in Leo**
8/16	**National Tell a Joke Day**
8/22	**Yod: Sun, Pluto, Saturn, Neptune**
8/22	**Sun enters Virgo, Happy birthday, Virgos!**
8/23	**New Moon at 0° Virgo,** read moon article
8/25	**Venus enters Leo**

RESOURCES

Numerology: 8 month in a 9 year

Gemstones: Iolite, Jade

Oils: Geranium, Patchouli

Rituals: Morning Reflection, Daily Planning, Keep Learning, Get Connected

Wisdom Diaries: Finding Balance Between Teaching & Learning

ORACLE PLAY

"What do I need to know about the month ahead?"

CARD 1   CARD 2   CARD 3   CARD 4   CARD 5

_____

_____

_____

_____

_____

Energy Almanac 2025 EDITION

♡ Fun, fresh, transformational products + services: https://choosebigchange.com ♡

AUGUST PREDICTIONS

MONDAY, AUGUST 4 – SUNDAY, AUGUST 10	MOONS: SCORPIO, SAGITTARIUS, CAPRICORN, AQUARIUS

With goals set last week you can leap into this one ready to roll and it begins Tuesday with a gorgeous Grand Trine in air signs. Grand Trines employ multiple planets all in the same element. This friendly transit brings opportunity involving education and the future, groups, perhaps frequency or AI as well as the legal system and peace-keeping efforts. Imagine the possibilities and use your sketchbook or journal to connect some dots. What generative possibility can be born from these topics? The next day...Mars, planet of action and aggression enters Libra, zodiac of relations and resources, which could bring you an urge for coupling over the next little while. Mars is masculine and Libra is ruled by Venus which is feminine. Both love and desire are present for the next many weeks. And Little Pretzel, there is more to come...

A kite in the cosmos between Mars in Libra, Pluto in Aquarius, Saturn in Aries, Neptune in Aries, and Uranus in Gemini bring you two grand trines connected. This benevolent energy brings some fated opportunity for change. Topics include partnership, innovation, proper use of leadership, as well as innovation and learning. There is plenty to work with and this aspect is typically benevolent. Let's all remember that everything is unfolding perfectly in spite of any unexpected shifts.

GIFT & SHADOW THIS WEEK: *With the Sun at Gate 7- Collaboration,cooperation, and co-creation are the gifts this week brings when we stop struggling to be seen and heard as "the leader." But the opposite may also be true. We may have dissolved so much into the group that we lost our individuality. This week, find the balance between teamwork and "me" work. As we evolve more and more consciousness, you will naturally find that middle ground where you are valued as much as you value the work of others. With Earth at Gate 13-Listening, part of the collaboration process is active listening when others are speaking. Remember that we are "collaborating," which means both parties share the listening/communicating aspects.*

FUN, FRESH, TRANSFORMATIONAL COMPANION PRODUCTS TO HELP MAKE 2025 AMAZING ARE AVAILABLE AT:

WWW.CHOOSEBIGCHANGE.COM

MONDAY, AUGUST 11 — SUNDAY, AUGUST 17

MOONS: PISCES, ARIES, TAURUS

On Monday morning Saturn in Aries tickles Uranus in Gemini and we are set up for a few days of contemplating leadership and learning. This could be about how we show up as teachers/leaders or how we might lead in the changing landscape of education. This sextile will last a handful of days and you can make notes about what you witness close to home and throughout the global arena. The rest of the week is set up for the influences of Aries (leadership and individuality) and Taurus (money and self-worth). Remember that we are in a year of curiosity. Keep asking yourself good questions and taking note of the answers. For fun, Saturday is National Tell A Joke Day. Did you hear about the man who entered the pet store who asked to buy a fish? The clerk said, "Do you want an aquarium?" The man replied, "I don't care about its astrology sign." Post your best astrology meme on social media Saturday. Be sure to tag us: @TheEnergyAlmanac.

GIFT & SHADOW THIS WEEK: *The Sun is at Gate 4-Logic this week, making it a time of possibility thinking! It is a "keep your options open" sort of energy. In the shadow, this can be self-doubt or the fear of not knowing. But if we can learn to let the power of possibilities stimulate our imaginations, then ideas become seeds of what more is possible in our lives and experiences. Possibilities are not yet truths, so we must wait until the truth is proven over time. Please don't shut down the possibilities because you are afraid they won't become truths. Open-mindedness is genuinely your ally!*

MONDAY, AUGUST 18 — SUNDAY, AUGUST 24

MOONS: GEMINI, CANCER, LEO, VIRGO

Things are heating up Little Pretzel. Friday brings another cosmic turning point when the sun in Leo , Pluto in Aquarius, Saturn and Neptune in Aries create a "yod" or "finger of God." This strong aspect typically creates an event worth remembering. This time potentials include your expression and passion as it relates to compassionate leadership and the transformation of groups. Remember to stay flexible as it unravels.

All of it occurs as The Sun enters Virgo and we celebrate are intelligent if not critical friends who are always interested in holistic health and workday routines. You can follow that up with a Saturday New Moon in Virgo gathering at the auspicious zero degree mark. This early morning moon (on the east coast) is a great time to reset your health goals. Learn even more about this moon by checking the article in the back of this month's resources.

GIFT & SHADOW THIS WEEK: *What are you committed to doing or being? With the Sun in Gate 29-Commitment this week, we get to explore what we say yes to and how we enter into our commitments. For some people, saying yes is automatic, and then when they realize they have said yes to too many things, half-hearted commitment ensues, or they have to back out of engagements. Of course, this can negatively impact our relationships and reputation. Saying yes requires us to use our intuition, body wisdom, or emotions to guide us to the correct things to say yes to. Then, the experience is magical. Jupiter moves into Gate 53-Starting Things this week as well. With the planet of expansion at this Gate, we will be very tempted to take on too much. Remember to say yes only to those things that are right for you!*

MONDAY, AUGUST 25 – SUNDAY, AUGUST 31

MOONS: VIRGO, LIBRA, SCORPIO

As August simmers down you can start the week with the pragmatic action of blocking time to review the last 30 days and your progress. Use your Virgo energy to its best capacity, friends. On Monday Venus enters Leo and passion is hot, hot, hot. There is fun in the air and an exuberance. Relationships could surely heat up and it's a good time to think about creative ways to make money. Be mindful of not being overly generous under this influence. Thursday the planets Uranus and Neptune are waltzing in the sky. Uranus is tackling education and Neptune is touring heart-centered leadership and individuality. Together they create a chance to innovate these topics. Expect some revelatory ideas that are flavored with spirituality. Bring those thoughts with you into the weekend as the Scorpio moon sprinkles mysticism into the mix. You are transforming the global landscape even if you think you are only influencing a small local number. Remember, as you transform, you automatically transform others creating a collective of people who are changed. Don't forget your month end review. Save goal setting for early September.

GIFT & SHADOW THIS WEEK: *The Sun and Earth help us deal with sustainability issues and enoughness this week. The Sun at Gate 59-Sustainability challenges us to choose from a state of abundance without fear of lack. In the shadow energy of this Gate, we feel like we have to struggle and fight to get our fair share and survive. The Earth at Gate 55-Abundance challenges us to have faith that we deserve to have more than enough to survive. Victim thinking stands as an old paradigm that we are in the process of releasing. When we release victimhood, we are free! It is a special kind of week when we can see that the gift of abundance is just a shift in thinking away.*

August Moon Work

AUGUST 9, 3:55 AM FULL MOON AT 17° AQUARIUS	○ **PASSIONATE ABOUT CHANGE**

The energy of this moon is laced with passion and "we energy." Rebellious Aquarius already prefers groups and with Mars in Libra aspected by Mercury, and outer planets Saturn, Uranus, Neptune, and Pluto the world is sure to to feel this moon. Expect leadership, innovation and transformation to be floating around your unconscious mind.

Uranus is also a strong player in this lunation. Suited in the button-down color-blocked shirt of Gemini, the planet of revelation is collaborating to bring insights and join those with the lower "thinking" mind that Mercury rules. This could make for creative ideas (Mercury is in Leo) that are helpful to the group (Pluto in Aquarius). Neptune is also playing nice with Uranus and Mercury. Together they are working on developing bold and compassionate moves.

The north node is aspected by Jupiter. To remind you, the north node is the collective sacred wound and represents our growth point. It's currently in the sign of Aries. Jupiter is in the intuitive sign of Cancer. Together they are encouraging a soulful and insightful approach to your autonomy. Don't be afraid of adding your own spiritual touches to your leadership style. You are encouraged to be brave enough to be seen "as you are." Your individuality is the perfect spice to this hot summer night we call a Full Moon. Set your intention to own your unique personality as it is and feel satisfied that it is working for the benefit of the world.

AFFIRMATION: *"I am willing and ready to stand tall and steady, my uniqueness is perfect."*

MOON WORK:

- Pull out your journal and write all the things that make you unique.
- Aquarians are intuitive. Spend time noticing the cosmic information that is coming to you under this moon.
- Identify where you have been afraid to be emotionally warm and vow to release that block and be more compassionate.

_____

_____

_____

_____

_____

_____

_____

_____

_____

♡ Fun, fresh, transformational products + services: https://choosebigchange.com ♡

AUGUST 23, 2:06 AM
NEW MOON AT 0° VIRGO

SERVICE TO SELF

This new moon in August in the practical sign of Virgo could be revelatory! Uranus, planet of disruption and brilliance has messages for you if you'll have them. Uranus is square the sun and moon bringing discomfort to the fore; it wants to innovate the social landscape while you may be yearning to stay home and do your good work. Only you know what is right for you, so choose accordingly. Uranus may deliver insights concerning your health, something all good Virgos enjoy working toward.

Mars is playing with Mercury and your mental capacities are tickled giving you an urge to play or be creative with a partner. It's probably a good choice for a warm summer night. If you're up for it, take your partner to any kind of playful outing before doing your intention setting in solitude.

The outer planets are working at a deep level across the planet. Jupiter will favor the use of intuition and wisdom but you may still be wanting to be less serious and just sink into a passionate night of romance. Your imagination will be quite strong with Neptune trine Venus, conjunct Saturn, and sextile Uranus. Apply your best Virgo logic to all imaginings to determine what intentions to set for the weeks ahead. If confusion sets in,because it might get cloudy, don't be afraid to bring order to your environment as a tool for gaining clarity.

AFFIRMATION: *"I am in service and in good standing with my higher self. I serve and I deserve a good life."*

MOON WORK:

- Do an inventory of your health to decide what intentions you want to include in your moon work today.
- Note confusion over the next day or so. Let the dust settle before making plans to address any of it.
- Your intuition is getting strong this year. Meditate on health, service, routines, and your own personal wisdom. Ask your higher self what you need to know that would help close a cycle for you.

_____

_____

_____

_____

_____

_____

_____

_____

_____

_____

_____

_____

Numerology

Numerologically this is an eight month in a nine year.
August = 8 and 2025 = 9; 8 + 9 = 17; 1 + 7 = 8

The number 8 is one of leadership, balance, and manifestation. In August you can use these subtle influences along with the acuity of the nine to lead as life requires. Trust wisdom gained from your past experiences to support your current leadership style.

Gemstones & Oils

GEMSTONES

Iolite Clears and enhances the third eye, improves empathy, inner vision, courage. It increases creativity, promotes a teamwork mindset, and instills hope during difficult times.

Jade Facilitates an abundance of energy flow, increases one's luck, eliminates bad thoughts. Jade promotes leadership, prosperity, improves relationships, removes toxic influences, relieves fear, irritability, and pain.

OILS

Geranium *Pelargonium graveolens*
Receptive, centering, creative, expressive
Blends well w/ Citrus, Frankincense, Cedarwood

Geranium helps center your nervous system, making self expression easier and flow with more grace. It empowers your personal sense of self and encourages creative play/work. It aids in opening up all your senses, leaving you more open minded, a better listener and more direct communicator. Geranium is wonderful to use when working with others in group settings, and for leadership.

Patchouli *Pogostemon cablin*
Enriching, arousing, harmonizing, balancing
Blends well w/ Rose, Geranium, Neroli, Orange, Clary Sage, Cedarwood

Patchouli helps to harmonize your mind and body, checking in to see where you may need reconnection, change, spice, or stimulation. Perfect for the over-worker who tends to take on too much at a time. Patchouli arouses all our senses, encouraging more creative self enrichment in our lives whether that be enrichment thru self love, picking up a new instrument, learning a new language or taking on a new project.

_____

_____

_____

_____

Rhythms, Routines & Rituals

Whether you're acing a test, mastering a new skill, or just dropping random knowledge bombs at parties, learning is your secret sauce. It's like flexing your mental muscles and becoming the superhero of your life. Navigate this month's energies with these routines:

- **Morning Reflection:** Start your day with a few minutes of reflection. Consider your goals for the day, prioritize tasks, and picture success in your mind. Keep our long-term goals handy and make it a habit to assess your progress daily.

- **Daily Planning:** Each morning, plan your day by identifying the three most important tasks and schedule time to complete them. (I have done this for many years and it is a game changer!)

- **Keep Learning:** This one bears repeating. It served you well in April and it doesn't go out of style. You can not go wrong by continuing to learn. If someone tells me they have ten years of experience, I always want to know if it's one year of experience repeated ten times, or has there been growth?

- **Get Connected:** Put yourself out there. Attend industry events, conferences, or networking sessions to build relationships and stay updated on trends in your field. Find a mom's group, a knitting circle or book club and meet some cool new friends.

If you're ready for a brand new rhythm, grab my bonus material.

_____

_____

_____

_____

_____

_____

_____

_____

_____

_____

GET YOUR FREE BONUS CONTENT AT:
WWW.CHOOSEBIGCHANGE.COM/PAGES/BONUS25

Scan here

�
 ✷ Get your book bonus offers: www.choosebigchange.com/pages/bonus25 ✷

Hey Uncle,

I hope this letter finds you in good health and high spirits. I've been doing some serious thinking about achieving balance between teaching and learning, and I couldn't think of anyone better to turn to for advice than you. With all your wisdom and experience, I know you've got some valuable insights to share.

You see, I've been in a bit of a quandary lately. On one hand, I'm eager to share what I know and help others grow and learn. But on the other hand, I don't want to come across as arrogant. How do you strike that delicate balance between being a teacher and being a learner? How do you stay humble while also stepping into a leadership role?

I've always admired how you manage to lead with grace and humility, never flaunting your knowledge or expertise but always willing to share it with others. It's a fine line to walk, and I'd love to hear your thoughts on how you've managed to do it so effectively.

Do you have any tips or strategies for staying humble while still stepping up as a leader? How do you ensure that you're always open to learning from others, even when you're the one in charge? And how do you handle situations where your knowledge or expertise is challenged without letting it affect your confidence or humility?

I know these are big questions, but I have faith that you'll have some valuable insights to share. Your guidance has always meant the world to me, and I'm grateful to have you as a mentor and role model. Looking forward to hearing your thoughts, Uncle.

Warm regards,
Your Niece/ Nephew

My dear Niece/Nephew,

It brings me great joy to receive your letter, and I'm honored that you would seek my advice on such important matters. Finding balance between teaching and learning, while also staying humble in a leadership role is indeed a journey that requires careful reflection and consideration.

First and foremost, let me assure you that you're already on the right track simply by being aware of the importance of humility and continuous learning. It's a sign of true wisdom to recognize that there is always more to learn, regardless of our level of expertise or experience.

One key aspect of staying humble while stepping into leadership is to maintain an attitude of openness and receptivity to new ideas and perspectives. Remember that everyone you encounter has something valuable to teach you, whether they're a seasoned expert or a newcomer to the field. Approach each interaction with curiosity and a willingness to listen, and you'll be amazed at how much you can learn from those around you.

At the same time, it's important to recognize and own your strengths and expertise without letting them go to your head. Confidence in your abilities is essential for effective leadership, but it should be tempered with humility and a recognition of your own limitations. Never be afraid to admit when you don't have all the answers or when you've made a mistake. Vulnerability can be a powerful tool for building trust and connection with those you lead.

Finally, remember that leadership is not about having all the answers or being the smartest person in the room. It's about empowering others to reach their full potential, fostering a culture of collaboration and mutual respect, and leading by example with integrity and authenticity. Stay true to your values, lead with empathy and compassion, and you'll find that humility naturally follows.

I hope these insights are helpful to you as you navigate the complexities of teaching, learning, and leadership. Remember that you have a wealth of support and wisdom within you and around you, and I have no doubt that you'll continue to grow and thrive on your journey.

With love and admiration,
Your Uncle

Month End Review

◇ ◆ ◇

What was new, good, and different about this month?

_____
_____
_____
_____
_____
_____
_____
_____
_____
_____
_____
_____
_____
_____
_____
_____
_____
_____
_____
_____
_____
_____
_____
_____
_____

September

PRACTICAL SPIRITUALITY

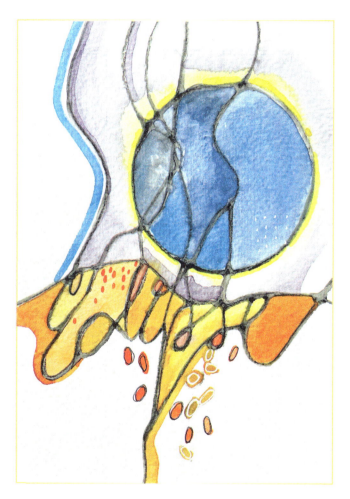

SEPTEMBER 1-7

DO capture all intuitive messages being received.
DO NOT fall victim to self-doubt.

SEPTEMBER 8-14

DO take time for extra self-care.
DO NOT forget to ask questions.

SEPTEMBER 15-21

DO block time for eclipse work.
DO NOT be close-minded.

SEPTEMBER 22-28

DO notice what in your life is transforming.
DO NOT avoid a month-end review.

WHAT IS THE BENEFIT OF APPLYING PRACTICALITY TO MY SPIRITUALITY?

SEPTEMBER 7, 2:09 PM

FULL MOON LUNAR ECLIPSE
AT 15° PISCES
INTUITIVE ORGANIZATION

SEPTEMBER 21, 3:54 PM

NEW MOON PARTIAL SOLAR ECLIPSE
AT 29° VIRGO
WISE AND WONDERFUL CHANGE

Energy Almanac 2025 EDITION

Month At-A-Glance

Write in the dates of this month before taking a few minutes to make notes of specific astrological time periods as they intersect with your own life happenings. You may even choose to highlight those time periods in green and red to remind yourself of easy and difficult days.

MONDAY	TUESDAY	WEDNESDAY	THURSDAY	FRIDAY	SATURDAY	SUNDAY

 Notes

September

—◇◈◇—

September offers many astrological opportunities. If you thought the last 30 days offered plenty, hold onto your shorts, Little Pretzel, September is loaded with activity. Of note is Saturn's retrograde in the compassionate, dreamy sign of Pisces and you can begin to review your own sense of discipline or lack thereof with spirituality and empathy. Practical thought processes and an analytical mind will help you navigate no less than five planetary yod's where the celestial bodies offer plenty of occasions for big change. Conflict is likely and the best you can do is remain flexible for the entire month of September. Stay on your toes and be reminded that the Full Moon Lunar Eclipse at 15 Pisces could be opening or closing doors for you and that in the end, it's all for the better. Flavor your thoughts with compassion for best results.

By mid-September a harmonious Grand Trine in air signs could bring respite and soften some of the edges from surprises from the yods occurring earlier in the month. Catch your breath because back-to-back-to-back aspecting planets September 19-22nd could be transformational. Your own personal urge for transformation is rampant too with Mars in Scorpio as the month winds down. The goal in September is to remain open to change and be adaptable. A glorious kite alignment helps us close the month. These typically easeful transits can illuminate new information to use for the rest of this year.

TRANSITS

9/1	**Saturn Retrograde in Pisces**
9/2	**Mercury enters Virgo**
9/2	**Yod: Mercury, Pluto, Neptune, Saturn**
9/6	**Uranus Retrograde in Gemini**
9/7	**Full Moon Total Lunar Eclipse at 15° Pisces**
9/14	**National Hug Your Hound Day**
9/17	**Yod: Saturn, Venus, Mars;**
9/17	**Arrowhead (Focused Yod), Saturn, Venus, Mercury, Mars**
9/18	**Grand Trine in Air Signs: Uranus, Mercury, Pluto**
9/18	**Mercury enters Libra**
9/19	**Venus enters Virgo**
9/19	**Arrowhead (Focused Yod) Saturn, Venus, Sun, Mars**
9/21	**New Moon Partial Solar Eclipse at 29° Virgo**

TRANSITS, CONT.

9/22	**Autumnal Equinox**
9/22	**Mars enters Scorpio**
9/22	**Kite: Sun, Pluto, Neptune, Saturn, Uranus**
9/22	**Sun enters Libra, Happy birthday, Librans!**

RESOURCES

Numerology: 9 month in a 9 year

Gemstones: Shiva Lingam, Malachite

Oils: Myrrh, Sandalwood

Rituals: Mindful Meals, Nature Connection, Random Acts of Kindness, Evening Reflection

Wisdom Diaries: Practices for Everyday Life

ORACLE PLAY

"What do I need to know about the month ahead?"

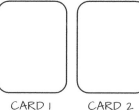 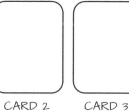   

CARD 1   CARD 2   CARD 3   CARD 4   CARD 5

_____

_____

_____

_____

_____

SEPTEMBER PREDICTIONS

MONDAY, SEPTEMBER 1 – SUNDAY, SEPTEMBER 7	**MOONS:** SAGITTARIUS, CAPRICORN, AQUARIUS

September starts with a soft roll as Saturn, planet of pressure, lessons, and karma, shifts retrograde in the compassionate sign of Pisces. This retrograde brings the opportunity to review how we collectively handled the seriousness of spirituality and compassion. Were you disciplined in your meditations and prayer? Did you push aside your gratitude lists and ignore your intuition? Tsk, tsk or tah-dah. Only you know how you did. The retrograde review period lasts through November. Hint: restart your gratitude list.

Tuesday the planetary reporter, Mercury, enters Virgo. This is a place he owns. It is his comfort zone to analyze, report, and then make judgment on what he knows. It's also a sweet place of pragmatism and genuine service to others. Mercury stays here only until September 18. Tap into the practical Virgo energy often. Also this day is another spectacular Yod meant to shake up the status quo. Here Mercury, Pluto, Neptune, and Saturn play and move to shift the world. Your only work is to stay open-minded.

Wednesday Jupiter in Cancer trines the North Node in Pisces and your intuition will be on high alert downloading all the messages you need. Watch for emotional overreactions and be okay if your vision suddenly expands into boundless realms you didn't know were possible. Be sure to capture what you take in for further introspection.

Lastly is Sunday's Full Moon Total Lunar Eclipse in Pisces which is absolutely certain to amplify and open your heart center. At the six degree mark notating love and more love, you will surely feel the feels under this lunation. Read more about it in this month's resource section which starts on page 133.

GIFT & SHADOW THIS WEEK: *The Earth is in Gate 63-Doubt this week. Remember, in Human Design, the Earth stands as a beacon of what we must ground into our reality to rise to the highest energy of the Sun. The Sun is at Gate 64-Illumination. Doubt isn't all bad. Without doubt, we wouldn't inquire and search for answers to some of life's biggest questions, and without inquiry we wouldn't reach enlightenment. Humanity has evolved due to the pressure doubt places upon us to answer those questions. The problem with doubt occurs when we internalize it into dogma, opinions, and beliefs to maintain a framework in our lives that makes sense—that keeps us from self-doubt. This week addresses the effect that self-doubt has had on your life. How has it shut down your process of questioning what you believe?*

_____

_____

_____

_____

_____

_____

_____

_____

_____

MONDAY, SEPTEMBER 8 – SUNDAY, SEPTEMBER 14

MOONS: PISCES, ARIES, TAURUS, GEMINI

Rest and take extra steps for self-care under the moon's lunations this week. Next week is astrologically loaded and we will all need to be prepared. For this week, dream, lead, work your harvest, and ask questions. Little Pretzel, Sunday is National Hug Your Hound Day. If your four-legged friend will let you, give him a warm hug from us as well. Tag a photo of you and your pup with @TheEnergyAlmanac.

GIFT & SHADOW THIS WEEK: *The Sun is in Gate 47-Mindset this week, which means we are dealing with the shadow of another mind-oriented issue: closed vs open-mindedness. With closed-mindedness, we rely on our attachment that answers will come to us in prescribed ways—likely through the intellect. The gift, however, reminds us that when we relinquish the mind's insistence on using intellect, magic can happen through epiphanies, aha's, and revelations. In an instant, the solution your mind has been working so hard on formulating breaks through with a solution. The key is to relax the mind and let the magic of the Universe work through you.*

MONDAY, SEPTEMBER 15 – SUNDAY, SEPTEMBER 21

MOONS: GEMINI, CANCER, LEO, VIRGO

As you read this article, set the intention that "all is well" and "all will be well." Astrology is nothing but a bunch of potentials and this week has many of them. It begins on Wednesday with yet another yod. Saturn, Venus, and Mars aspect one another to create a fast change. Yod's are the "finger of God." Here we simply wish to alert you to something shifting, potentially in the area of leadership (Saturn in Aries). Venus in Leo means passion is present and Mars in Libra could add the much needed temperance. Is the leader you or on someone at a societal level? Take notes in the days that follow. And if that isn't enough, hold on for Thursday when a Grand Trine comes to our rescue in air signs. Uranus in Gemini, Mercury in Libra, and Pluto in Aquarius suggest that education, balance or legalities, and the good of the group are at play. It is sure to soften whatever the yod hoped to create. On the same day as the trine Mercury enters Libra to bring balance to our thoughts and our budget. You could find yourself hyper-critical inside of relations, so be mindful of that and use your words wisely. Little Pretzel, you're only through Thursday.

Friday brings a shift for Venus. Imagine Marilyn Monroe wearing a lab coat. Practical expressions of love are in play. If you're suddenly willing to do the laundry so your partner doesn't need to, don't be shocked. Do write us an email so we can have a giggle. Also Friday is another, say it with me, yod. Yes, another potential turning point. Saturn in Aries, Venus in Leo, the Sun in Virgo and Mars in Libra. We shall collectively see what comes to a head when this cosmic rumble occurs.

On Saturday (Saturn day) stay the course and handle your tasks as any good Pretzel would; on Sunday the New Moon Partial Eclipse in Virgo at the anaretic 29th degree is upon us along with a yod. It seems the universe has something big to say to us this year considering the same day a yod serves up Mars in Libra, Neptune in Aries, Saturn in Aries, and Uranus in Gemini. This moon could be a doozy as the 29th degree is a crisis point of sorts and this time it involves routine, service, health and a practical approach to life. The yod could spark hostilities. What a great time for creating lasting change if we remain pliable. Read more about this moon in this month's Moon Work section on page 134.

GIFT & SHADOW THIS WEEK: *The Sun is in Gate 6-Conflict Resolution, while the Earth is in Gate 36-Turbulence this week. We are working toward peace, and it turns out it is an inside job. You have heard that at one time or another. This week's energy really brings that message home as the shadow energies of conflict and turbulence surface for us collectively and individually. These energies are the primary source of war. Yet, war usually begins in the collective mind, where we may fear not having enough resources or other similarly incorrect assumptions. The pathway to peace on the planet resides in the effort that each of us puts into finding peace within ourselves, compassion for ourselves and others, and remembering our shared humanity.*

MONDAY, SEPTEMBER 22 – SUNDAY, SEPTEMBER 28

MOONS: LIBRA, SCORPIO, SAGITTARIUS

Monday, September 22, opens the final full week of this month as the planet of action, Mars, pulls on a black hoodie and ties that hood tightly around his face creating a strong urge for personal transformation. As your mind moves to the mysteries you may find yourself seeking rituals and exploring life and death while in the sky planets form a kite. This auspicious alignment brings amazing opportunities for growth. This happens on the same day that the Sun enters Libra. The kite can open ways for people to access their talents. With Pluto, Sun in Virgo, Neptune and Saturn in Aries, and Uranus in Gemini playing it could bring some practicality to learning and leadership. With the Sun in Libra through mid-October notice your passivity in relationships and a willingness to keep the peace. Be sure you're standing down at the right times and employing heart-centered leadership equally.

Is September over yet? Wow. Take a selfie with your well loved and tattered Energy Almanac. We want to see what the month of September looks like. Tag us: @TheEnergyAlmanac

GIFT & SHADOW THIS WEEK: *We have arrived at the turning of the seasons, which represents the evolution of our consciousness through the year. At this time of the year, we are tasked to begin expressing, in the physical world, the things we have learned about ourselves. How have your experiences thus far created challenges and/or learning experiences? In grounding in the learning and evolution we have been through, we are urged to remember that we are of Divine nature. We are explorers utilizing the 3D Earthly experience to evolve our consciousness, which is primarily of Spirit. This is a week to love yourself fully, no matter how well your mind thinks it has done in the year so far.*

_____

_____

_____

_____

_____

_____

_____

September Moon Work

SEPTEMBER 7, 2:09 PM
FULL MOON TOTAL LUNAR ECLIPSE
AT 15° PISCES

INTUITIVE ORGANIZATION

One of summer's last moons is upon you with the Sun is in Virgo and the moon is in Pisces creating a beautiful, flowing Pisces full moon lunar eclipse. Your thinking mind will be encouraging practical application of everything you touch and you may find yourself reordering or codifying your world while a part of you wants to lay around eating bon-bons and dreaming about the next best bon-bon. It's likely you'll be able to intuit how to best arrange your home environment for better flow thanks to Grandmother Moon and cheerleader Jupiter's help. With your expanded wisdom applied in a practical manner you can determine what to keep and what to throw out, where you can simplify decor, and encourage growth. Don't be surprised if you can hear the whispering of your grandmother as you hold objects and decide if they stay or go but do be mindful of your partner's needs, too. Mars in Libra may make things feisty.

Uranus is still sextile retrograde Saturn. This encourages your intuition in a big way. With the moon, Jupiter, Uranus, Neptune and Saturn all tickling your higher mind and second sight could provide some good albeit surprising information for you to work with. And every good Virgo loves to be productive, even if it is only in the mind.

Transformation of the group and the ways in which we innovate and use digital technology are only beginning to play out. This moon triggers Pluto, Uranus, and Neptune again encouraging silent information that will light up your world. Your job is to not get lost in escapism and overwhelm, but to instead make note of what's coming to you and work with the insight once you're done with the bon-bons.

AFFIRMATION: *"I know, I flow, I love and I grow and it's a beautiful thing."*

MOON WORK:

- Block time for work and play. You'll feel interested in bringing order, so do that, but also allow time for creative dreaming.
- Pisces are compassionate and emotional beings. Allow your emotion to fill your heart.
- Martyrdom and escapism can be problematic. Before setting any intentions this month, be honest with yourself and discover what you're using as a tool to escape or avoid reaching your life goals. Determine to be done with that!

_____

_____

_____

_____

_____

_____

_____

_____

♡ Fun, fresh, transformational products + services: https://choosebigchange.com ♡

SEPTEMBER 21, 3:54 PM
NEW MOON PARTIAL SOLAR ECLIPSE AT 29° VIRGO

 WISE AND WONDERFUL CHANGE

And here it is, on the Fall Equinox, a spectacular new moon solar eclipse ready and willing to open and close doors in your world as it relates to service, health, and routines. It begins with the sun and moon holding hands with Mercury in the sign of Libra making you an extremely intelligent, service-driven, diplomatic and passionate being. You may be ripe for a good review of your spiritual practices with Saturn retrograde but there's a little battle between doing a review and sticking to your more physical routine. Here's hoping you find time to do both.

Pay special attention to the underlying messaging that is happening in the greater world because the planets are extremely busy during this eclipse. Start by expecting Uranus to bring insights to you on the topics of social media, networking, education and your own sociability. Warning! Neptune opposing the sun, moon, and Mercury could cloud those insights making them feel slightly out of reach as though you know there's something to know but you just can't put your finger on it, you know? Hang in there because Uranus is actually well aspected to Neptune to encourage the revelations and add a flavor of love to whatever is going on. This could make the information easier to read. You may note feeling bolstered toward leadership as an act of service to the world. If so, go for it!

Pluto is working to put your attention on the group again. Good Virgo that you are for today, ask how you can be of service to others, many, many others and how might that be activated? The weeks that follow should provide some clarity to that. Again, your partner may not want to play along so adding diplomacy will be important as you work through the results of this eclipse. Pluto is working harmoniously with Uranus and Neptune to give you both information and imagination as to how this could play out. There's clearly plenty on the table to digest under this eclipse so keep your journal very nearby.

Your tool this month is wisdom. Tap into it what it means to be a strong, soul-fueled leader who knows just what to do next. Opportunities will arise and when they do apply good Virgo practical logic to them and step forward into change.

AFFIRMATION: *"I am aligned with wisdom. I know just what to do and when to do it."*

MOON WORK:

- Keep a good journal for a week. Pay attention to what you learn from your thoughts and note opportunities. Eclipses create change. The notetaking will help you analyze the opportunities.
- Health is always on the mind of Virgo, it's a great time to set an intention for increasing your own vitality. In good Virgo form, keep your routines simple.
- Meditate on the topic of service to discover where you can be of the highest and best use to the world.

_____

_____

_____

_____

_____

_____

Numerology

Numerologically this is a nine month in a nine year.
September = 9 and 2025 = 9; 9 + 9 = 18; 1 + 8 = 9

September is set up to be an auspicious month of completion and transformation. You have "been there, done that" and this month you may feel the fullness of the education life has given you. Apply it wisely.

Gemstones & Oils

GEMSTONES

Shiva Lingam Increases vitality and pranic energy, stimulates the entire body and energy system, aids fatigue and fertility. Connects with all chakras, and assists in Sacred meditations and kundalini activation.

Malachite Strengthens intuition and instinct, uncovers repressed emotions, absorbs negative energy. It activates swift positive transformation, harmonizes the emotional body—especially the heart, and helps you resist temptations.

OILS

Myrrh *Commiphora myrrha*
Transcending, spiritual, solitude
Blends well w/ Clary Sage, Lavender, Frankincense, Lemon, Vetiver

Myrrh, like Sandalwood, is known to enhance spirituality. Helpful when one needs to shake up their spiritual connection and separate from the mundane of life, by lessening overthinking, ruminating thoughts that get in the way of spiritual connections. Myrrh encourages solitude to reconnect to our mind, body and heart.

Sandalwood *Santalum album*
Spiritual, transforming, stillness
Blends well w/ Ylang Ylang, Rose, Lavender, Black Pepper, Grapefruit

Sandalwood's repertoire of being the perfect oil to use for meditation is due to its toning nature of the nervous system. It brings about feelings of calm and stillness where the answers one may be seeking from the divine are easily received, absorbed and transformed into action. Sandalwood encourages us to partake in spiritual routines. The timeless wisdom that Sandalwood provides engulfs one with a compassionate self-worth and confidence.

_____

_____

_____

_____

♡ Fun, fresh, transformational products + services: https://choosebigchange.com ♡

Rhythms, Routines & Rituals

Integrating spiritual practices doesn't have to be all woo-woo, try these simple routines to enhance your spirituality in practical ways.

- **Mindful Meals:** Practice mindfulness during meals by savoring each bite, expressing gratitude for your food, and being present in the moment. Aim to eat at least one meal each day with complete attention, avoiding distractions like screens. And don't forget to chew, chew, chew!

- **Nature Connection:** Get outside, whether it's a daily walk, weekend hike, or sitting in a park. This does wonders for your mood and energy. I stop by the beach as often as possible. Remember, there is no bad weather, only bad clothing.

- **Random Acts of Kindness:** Perform small, intentional acts of kindness for others without expecting anything in return. Create a game of making kindness a regular part of your life and aim to delight and surprise!

- **Evening Reflection:** Reflect on your day, acknowledging both challenges and successes. Self-reflection before bedtime allows you to learn and grow from your experiences. This may be a good time for reading spiritual texts, sacred scriptures, or inspirational books.

When we tune into the rhythm in our bodies, in our hearts and in our lives—no matter where we are or what our circumstances are, we are invited to take a moment to pause. We stop running, stop achieving, stop doing, and find rhythm in our life throughout the year. Check out my bonus material for more rituals like these.

_____

_____

_____

_____

_____

_____

_____

_____

_____

GET YOUR FREE BONUS CONTENT AT:
WWW.CHOOSEBIGCHANGE.COM/PAGES/BONUS25

Scan here

Wisdom Diaries

Dear Mom,

I've been feeling a strong pull towards exploring my personal spirituality more deeply in my everyday life. I know that you've always had a strong connection to the divine, and I was wondering if you could share some specific practices that I can incorporate into my daily routine.

I'm looking for tangible actions that can help me feel more grounded, centered, and connected to something greater than myself. Whether it's meditation, prayer, journaling, or something else entirely, I'm open to exploring different avenues and finding what resonates most with me.

I admire the way you embrace your sacredness with such grace and reverence, and I trust your guidance in this area. I believe that incorporating spiritual practices into my daily life can bring a sense of peace, clarity, and purpose that I've been longing for.

If you're willing, I would love to hear about any specific practices that you've found particularly meaningful or transformative in your own spiritual journey. How do you incorporate spirituality into your daily life, and what benefits have you experienced as a result?

Thank you for always being a source of wisdom and inspiration for me. I'm grateful to have you as my guide as I continue to explore this beautiful journey of self-discovery and spiritual growth.

> With love and gratitude,
> Your Child

My Dearest Child,

It warms my heart to hear that you are feeling the call to deepen your spiritual connection and explore new practices to incorporate into your daily life. Your journey into the co-creative process with the Divine is a beautiful path to embark on and I am more than happy to share some practices that have been meaningful to me.

First and foremost, I want to encourage you to trust your intuition and explore practices that resonate with you personally. Spirituality is a deeply personal journey, and what works for one person may not necessarily work for another. That being said, here are a few practices that I have found to be particularly transformative:

- **Meditation:** Taking even just a few minutes each day to sit in stillness and quiet the mind can have profound effects on your overall well-being. Whether you prefer guided meditations, mindfulness practices, or simply focusing on your breath, find a meditation technique that feels comfortable and accessible to you.

- **Gratitude Journaling:** Cultivating an attitude of gratitude can shift your perspective and bring more joy and abundance into your life. Each day, take a few moments to write down three things that you are grateful for. It can be something as simple as a beautiful sunset or a kind gesture from a friend.

- **Nature Connection:** Spending time in nature is a powerful way to connect with something greater than yourself and to feel a sense of awe and wonder. Whether it's going for a walk in the park, sitting by the ocean, or simply gazing at the stars, make time to immerse yourself in the beauty of the natural world.

- **Prayer or Affirmations:** Engaging in prayer or repeating positive affirmations can help you cultivate a sense of faith and trust in the universe. Whether you pray to a higher power, speak words of affirmation to yourself, or simply set intentions for the day ahead, these practices can help you align with your highest good.

Remember, my dear, that spirituality is a journey, not a destination. Be patient and gentle with yourself as you explore these practices and allow yourself to evolve and grow along the way. I am here to support you every step of the way and to cheer you on as you continue to deepen your spiritual connection.

> With all my love,
> Your Momma

♡ Fun, fresh, transformational products + services: https://choosebigchange.com ♡

Month End Review

What was new, good, and different about this month?

_____

_____

_____

_____

_____

_____

_____

_____

_____

_____

_____

_____

_____

_____

_____

_____

_____

_____

_____

_____

_____

_____

_____

_____

October

WATCH THE WATERS

SEPTEMBER 29–OCTOBER 5

DO demonstrate what you know.
DO NOT be so practical in your vision
for yourself.

OCTOBER 6–12

DO check your financial resources.
DO NOT be afraid to face what may
be coming.

OCTOBER 13–19

DO primp your home environment.
DO NOT fall prey to failure thinking.

OCTOBER 20–26

DO be clear when teaching others.
DO NOT allow confusion to derail you.

OCTOBER 27–NOVEMBER 2

DO make life a joyful adventure.
DO NOT avoid a month-end review.

WHAT WOULD IT TAKE TO ALLOW DEEP EMOTIONAL HEALING THIS MONTH?

OCTOBER 6, 11:47 PM

FULL MOON AT 14° ARIES
LISTEN BEFORE LEAPING

OCTOBER 21, 8:25 AM

NEW MOON AT 28° LIBRA
PARTNERING WITH CHANGE

Energy Almanac · 2025 EDITION

♡ Love the Energy Almanac? Tag us on social media: @TheEnergyAlmanac ♡

Page 139

Month At-A-Glance

Write in the dates of this month before taking a few minutes to make notes of specific astrological time periods as they intersect with your own life happenings. You may even choose to highlight those time periods in green and red to remind yourself of easy and difficult days.

MONDAY	TUESDAY	WEDNESDAY	THURSDAY	FRIDAY	SATURDAY	SUNDAY

Notes

October

◇◇◇

October is both warm and wild, happy and haunting, too. Bright oranges, reds, and golds paint the landscape as pumpkins with strange faces pop up everywhere. This year October holds a week that has three, yes three, grand trines. Our early advice is to breathe deep the first three weeks before the ride that happens from October 20-26. The after-effects can be wonderful as humanity shifts in many ways. Keep your expectations high and lean into your own vision of a kinder, more loving society where it truly is all for one and one for all.

Mysticism will be on your mind as well as transformation under the multiple Scorpio transits. Alchemy seems urgent every October and the planets sure want to deliver through the lens of two grand trines the last full week of the month. Neptune will go retrograde in Pisces. You'll end the year wondering if you actively participated in your own spirituality or chose escapism instead. The Grand Trines in water signs are for healing. If you've never reached for emotional healing tools before or had an emotional support person, this could be the month to employ them. Remember that though soul-stirring, there is nothing to be afraid of as the Universe has your back and everything is unfolding perfectly.

TRANSITS

10/3	**World Smile Day**
10/6	**Mercury enters Scorpio**
10/6	**Full Moon at 14° Aries,** read moon article
10/13	**Venus enters Libra**
10/13	**Pluto direct in Aquarius**
10/21	**New Moon at 28° Libra,** read moon article
10/22	**Neptune Retrograde in Pisces**
10/22	**Sun enters Scorpio, Happy birthday, Scorpios!**
10/22	**Grand Trine in Water Signs: Jupiter, Mercury, Saturn**
10/25	**Grand Trine in Water Signs: Jupiter, Mars, Mercury, and Saturn**
10/26	**Grand Trine in Water Signs: Jupiter, Mars, Saturn**
10/29	**Mercury enters Sagittarius**

RESOURCES

Numerology: 10 month in a 9 year

Gemstones: Aquamarine, Chiastolite/Andalusite

Oils: Cedarwood, Eucalyptus

Rituals: Smooth Sailing

Wisdom Diaries: Deep Emotional Healing

ORACLE PLAY

"What do I need to know about the month ahead?"

CARD 1   CARD 2   CARD 3   CARD 4   CARD 5

_____

_____

_____

_____

_____

♡ Fun, fresh, transformational products + services: https://choosebigchange.com ♡

OCTOBER PREDICTIONS

MONDAY, SEPTEMBER 29 – SUNDAY, OCTOBER 5	MOONS: SAGITTARIUS, CAPRICORN, AQUARIUS, PISCES

Monday brings the end of the month and the first thing you can do on Monday or Tuesday is your regular month end review before setting new October goals. Wednesday you may find your nose to the grindstone under the Capricorn moon and you slide into the weekend with the potential for many intuitive downloads and thoughts of the future. It's a gentle week with Friday ending the work week on National Smile Day. Be sure to flash one to everyone you meet. Then, if time permits, spend it dwelling on the lunar nodes. Pisces is the collective way forward. How can you use compassion, empathy, creativity, and your visioning capacity to build a brighter future? Virgo is the collective history indicating what we can leave behind. How can you be less critical and less practical in your visioning of the future? Where can you stop playing the martyr or victim? Such good food for thought. Your journal should be pretty full these days.

GIFT & SHADOW THIS WEEK: *We are in the midst of a 7-week process of releasing fears of the False Evidence Appearing Real kind (F.E.A.R.). This process ramps up every year at this time as the Sun moves through the Gates of the Spleen Center in our Human Design. The Spleen is the center for time, intuition, and survival. All the gates in the spleen can double as gates of fear or paralysis. We face inadequacy as a shadow this week. Inadequacy can propel us into struggling to know more and more before we ever do anything with our gifts and talents. We have forgotten that there is a deep well of wisdom within us just waiting to be brought to the surface of our waking mind. This is an excellent week to demonstrate what you know. Dare to face the fear that you're not good enough or don't know enough. One more certification isn't going to make that fear disappear, but practicing your knowledge in the real world will. To quote a famous line, "just do it!"*

_____

_____

MONDAY, OCTOBER 6 – SUNDAY, OCTOBER 12	MOONS: ARIES, TAURUS, GEMINI

The second week of the month opens with the planetary reporter, Mercury, moving into the mysterious sign of Scorpio. Note over the next few weeks as your language is brushed with intensity and passion. At the same time, you may be coming from a more logical than emotional standpoint. This transit lasts for most of the rest of October. Mercury's move happens just hours before the Full Moon in Aries. Catch up on the meaning of this initiating moon in our resources section this month. The moon article is on page 146. The rest of your week moves you through Taurus and then Gemini influences. Use Wednesday and Thursday for checking the budget and earnings potential then use the weekend for socializing or learning.

GIFT & SHADOW THIS WEEK: *We face the fear of the future this week with the Sun at Gate 57-Intuition. Working with this shadow means facing what might be coming even if we don't know how the wind blows. This is primarily about instinctual awareness—the intuition and body wisdom for surviving and thriving. Unfortunately, we have given over too much power to the mind and have lost that connection. We now see the future with some trepidation or anxiety because we are trying to use the mind to "figure out" what to do. Reconnect with your body's wisdom as it is still there, a ready tool for you to use to determine what the next steps are for you.*

_____

_____

MONDAY, OCTOBER 13 – SUNDAY, OCTOBER 19	MOONS: CANCER, LEO, VIRGO, LIBRA

It's another light astrology week, friends. Monday brings Venus' move into Libra. Imagine Marilyn Monroe all beautiful in her white sequined dress and high heels. All love and money she is! That's Venus in Libra, comfortable working on relationships, peace keeping, and abundance. Notice over the next few weeks your attention to aesthetics, money, and coupling of all kinds. It could be a good time to primp yourself or your home environment. New sheets seem like a nice idea, too. The influence lasts through mid-November. Returning to this week, you can set your sights on first homelife, then creative expression, practical routines, and…saving the best for last, a weekend focused on time together. It's a great Saturday to cuddle, watch movies, and hang out. With the autumn colors so vibrant perhaps plan a romantic getaway at a cabin in the woods. Take a picture of you and your partner and tag us. @TheEnergyAlmanac Rest up. Next week is a doozy.

GIFT & SHADOW THIS WEEK: *We face the fear of failure this week. Or is it the fear of success? Either way, we get to address the impact of failure-thinking and success-aversion this week. There is no such thing as failure, or not, in the sense that we humans allow it to affect us. Instead, failure is a blip on the screen telling us that something needs to be tweaked or changed to move forward. Sometimes, we get in our own way of success, slowing down the process because we might fear who we would be without the struggle. Yikes—let it all go this week. Do you in spectacular fashion.*

_____

_____

_____

_____

_____

Stay On Top of Your Emotional Game

MORNING MAGIC

Sweet Spot

M + B + S = :)

THE DAILY MANIFESTIVAL IS A 30-DAY DIY **SPIRITUAL JUMPSTART** EMAIL COURSE THAT INCLUDES ALIGNING, BELIEF BUSTING, AND CULTIVATING A PLAN FOR FLOW.

Go to choosebigchange.com and enter "manifestival" in the search bar.

♡ Fun, fresh, transformational products + services: https://choosebigchange.com ♡

MONDAY, OCTOBER 20 – SUNDAY, OCTOBER 26

MOONS: LIBRA, SCORPIO, SAGITTARIUS

The antics begin on Tuesday the 21st under the New Moon in Libra. If you took our advice last week and spent time coupling over the weekend then you may have some fresh ideas about what you want from love and/or money. Set a new 30 day goal and use our moon article on page 147 to guide it. Wednesday we celebrate our Scorpio friends and we individually begin to carry an edge of mystery and passion. As Neptune, the bringer of compassion and faith begins his journey retrograde in the sign of Pisces, your thoughts turn inward and true soul searching begins. There could be some confusion, but don't allow it to derail you. It's a long term transit ending in early December. Humpday brings even more. It's the first of three Grand Trines in water signs that will happen this week. Wednesday involves Jupiter, Mercury, and Saturn. Zodiacs of the water signs ensure you plenty of emotional healing. The second and third of these benevolent transits occur on Saturday and Sunday. What we want to warn you is that emotions may run high and that tears wash away what doesn't serve. Feel it to heal it. You decide what "it" actually is.

Let's jump back to Thursday when Jupiter, the great expander, in Cancer, sign of homelife, intuition, and emotion square the collective sacred leadership wound. Chiron in Aries has brought leadership, individuality, and boldness to the fore. On Thursday you may feel that the wound is bigger than you can handle. Considering the emotional energy packed into these seven days, stay grounded, have tools (and tissues) ready.

Remember that though emotional, there is nothing to be afraid of as the Universe has your back and everything is unfolding perfectly.

GIFT & SHADOW THIS WEEK: *The Sun is in Gate 50- Values this week. Gate 50 is part of the feminine half of the Tribal Circuitry in Human Design, the purpose of which is to teach the values of the "tribe" with love. But sometimes, the information taught gets corrupted. Did you ever play telephone as a kid and pass a message down the line only to discover that the last person has a corrupted version of the original message? That is what we are dealing with this week—corruption. Code corruptions happen frequently in the computer world, and we, as people, are also susceptible to misreading the information we receive. But, when we slow down enough to really listen), we can ensure the message is pure and nurtured lovingly. Be clear about what you teach others, either directly or indirectly.*

ENERGY ALMANAC CHALLENGE: Write this phrase twenty times in your journal: "Everything is unfolding perfectly, the Universe has my back." Take a picture of your writing and post on IG; tag us so we can send you good mojo.

MONDAY, OCTOBER 27 – SUNDAY, NOVEMBER 2

MOONS: CAPRICORN, AQUARIUS, PISCES

Monday opens the week with a sense of seriousness under a Capricorn moon and Wednesday Mercury pulls on the worn out logo t-shirt of adventurous Sagittarius. While thoughts move toward your own personal theology a lightness is about and you could find yourself planning some adventures. Use your analytical brain to grab exactly the right train at the right time for the right destination as any good Sag would. You have through November to be mindful that not everybody appreciates the truth-telling that can occur under this influence.

Friday is America's Halloween. If you celebrate this holiday then we say "Boo!" to you and heartily giggle at your costume. The weekend is flavored with laying around and using your intuition to determine the best hiding spot for the Snickers®. Send the candy corns to our publisher! Seriously though, insights could come quickly under the Aquarius and Pisces moons. Use them as you do your month end review and set new objectives for November.

Don't forget to change the clocks on Saturday night before hitting the hay. Fall back one more time.

GIFT & SHADOW THIS WEEK: *We are closing in on the last week of the Sun's transit through the Gates on the Spleen Center, where fears and shadows can create paralysis in our lives. This week, we confront our fear of death through Gate 28-Struggle. We must not let struggle and challenge defeat us or make us feel like life is not worth living. Sometimes, it's the purposelessness we feel when life's events feel heavy and difficult. Make life an adventure. See challenges as something that elevates your life or uplevels your consciousness. We know we are all going to die someday, but life's challenges are not meant to get us there sooner. Find purpose, meaning, and love by sharing your experiences with others.*

_____

_____

_____

_____

_____

_____

♡ Fun, fresh, transformational products + services: https://choosebigchange.com ♡

October Moon Work

LISTEN BEFORE LEAPING

The bright October full moon comes with some tension, friend. Magnifier Jupiter in the sign of emotional and intuitive Cancer is square the sun and moon creating a battle between being wise and being bold. The natural desire to lead and do what you need to is conflicted. Some part of you is saying, "think this through—what can you look at from personal history that might foretell how this will play out?" Be aware to not leap before listening!

Jupiter is playing kindly with Venus in Virgo and a practical partnership could benefit from your expended intuition or maybe there's just some strong emotion between you, either way, emotions run strong. Could it be a good moon for generating abundance? Use the partnership of Saturn and Jupiter to reflect on manifestation practices that have helped you in the past. Inspiration could strike and then you can create a simple plan toward achieving the goal you set under the New Moon eclipse in September.

Your imagination could be boundary-free or currently cloudy, but listen carefully for information that could agitate things, Uranus is in the sandbox with Saturn who is retrograde in Pisces helping you to use your imagination and creativity. There's nothing like a little information that's spicy to flavor your world.

Finally, Pluto. He's bringing thoughts of transformation to you personally and poking you to think about how your own shifts might apply to the congregation. He is generating questions and triggering new data for you to download.

It's a lot to manage under one full moon. Your main focus should always be on how you can improve you for the greater "we." If that's all you do tonight, you will have done well.

AFFIRMATION: *"I am willing to act boldly after listening inward carefully."*

MOON WORK:

- Listen before you leap. Take some time to examine your personal history by remembering times you lept before listening. What is the lesson there?
- Study the tarot card of the Fool to better understand Aries energy.
- Reflect on the previous two weeks since the eclipse What is changing or where have you been presented opportunities? Reread this article and see what is applicable.

_____
_____
_____
_____
_____
_____

OCTOBER 21, 8:25 AM
NEW MOON AT 28° LIBRA

PARTNERING WITH CHANGE

The weather is crisp and in your heart peace reigns supreme, but it's not without some tension between what's changing within large groups and how you might apply your leadership skills there. Top of mind are the mysteries of the world and of your own recent changes. Passion is building and your intuition is loud. Everything is pointing to the simmering urge to be okay in your own skin exactly as you are. A peaceful heart starts at home and your work is to love yourself so that you can be a confident leader. This moon helps with all of that.

Wisdom, if you will let it, will find you. Jupiter is growing your discernment. Mars is helping you take action toward your own evolution, and the north node is cheering you on.

The new moon is not without global conditions as the large outer planets play together to develop soulful people who care for each other. There's work to do, for sure, but it isn't without great reward.

Uranus, Neptune, and Pluto are waltzing across the cosmos tugging at each other. They are encouraging innovation, imagination, and change. It's likely if you listen carefully you'll know exactly what they're moving you toward. Set your intentions toward a peaceful heart that loves you first.

AFFIRMATION: *"I am the perfect partner for me. I love who I am and prosper accordingly."*

MOON WORK:

- Avoid complacency when it comes to learning self-love. The best partner you have in life is you and your confidence. Mirror work is a great starting point.
- Wisdom remains a major topic in 2025. It's a wonderful time to review your notebook to see what wisdom you've collected so far this year.
- Talk with your partner about the changes you've noticed in them. Compliment their growth!

_____

_____

_____

_____

_____

_____

_____

_____

_____

_____

_____

_____

Numerology

Numerologically this is a ten month in a nine year.
October = 10 and 2025 = 9; 10 + 9 = 19; 1 + 9 = 10

Ten is the chance to start again. This number is initiating in nature and includes some level of inspiration or intuition. Transformation, from the nine, has given you sagacity. Apply that to the next journey and it's sure to serve you well.

Gemstones & Oils

GEMSTONES

Aquamarine Promotes perseverance, truth telling, calm and cool communication. Regulates hormones, reduces stress, sharpens perception and intuition, counteracts darkness, lessens grief and clutter. Protects you during travel, especially in water.

Chiastolite/Andalusite Connected to Earth energy, dispels and protects against negative energies. Activates problem solving, helps ground the physical body, allows one to be aware of changes, and brings harmony.

OILS

Cedarwood *Cedrus atlantica*
Endurance, knowing
Blends well w/ Bergamot, Eucalyptus, Lavender, Rosemary, Geranium

Cedarwood's strong aroma is no different than her subtle energetics, she is strong and can endure many obstacles. Cedarwood has an unwavering knowing of life, and will assist you in your most challenging situations by igniting your drive, determination and will. It assists you to accept what cannot be changed and what is to come. Her ability to calm your mind and avoid pessimism brings feelings of balance and the ability to hear your inner self without conflict.

Eucalyptus *Eucalyptus globulus*
Refresh, optimism, drive
Blends well w/ Lemon, Ginger, Fir, Peppermint, Basil, Cedarwood

Eucalyptus is highly antibacterial and the same way it knocks out germs, it knocks down barriers in the way due to fear, excess caution, and hesitation. It is a great oil to use to balance the bright refreshing parts of life with the hurdles we all endure. One moment Eucalyptus has you cleaning, scheduling, organizing your life in practical ways, the next moment she is swiftly tackling barriers and making new pathways you never knew existed. She cleanses your inner house so that you may shine more freely on the outside.

_____

_____

Rhythms, Routines & Rituals

Let's try a Smooth Sailing Ritual to navigate this month's turbulence in style.

- **Set the Scene:** Choose a quiet and comfortable space. Light a candle or use soft lighting to create a soothing atmosphere. Have paper, pen and a small bowl of water handy.

- **Breathing Exercise:** Begin with deep, intentional breaths. Inhale slowly, feeling the breath fill your lungs, and exhale, releasing tension. Focus on your breath to bring your awareness to the present moment.

- **Cleansing Visualization:** Envision a calming body of water, symbolizing your emotions. Imagine any negativity or turbulence being carried away by the gentle current, leaving you cleansed and free.

- **Symbolic Release:** Write down emotions or thoughts weighing heavy on you. Place the paper into the bowl of water, symbolizing your willingness to release and let go.

- **Healing Affirmations:** Affirm your strength, resilience, and capacity for healing with affirmations such as:

    - "I am deserving of love, healing, and inner peace."

    - "I release all that no longer serves me, and I embrace healing and renewal."

- **Reflective Journaling:** Jot down your feelings and thoughts in a journal.

- **Candle Visualization:** Focus on the candle's flame as a source of inner strength and warmth, dispelling darkness and guiding you through choppy emotional waters.

- **Closing:** Place your hands on your heart. Visualize a serene, calm sea, symbolizing emotional peace. Absorb the tranquility and carry it with you beyond the ritual.

You're now sailing on smooth waters! For more healing rituals to recalibrate, check out my bonus material.

_____

_____

_____

_____

_____

GET YOUR FREE BONUS CONTENT AT:
WWW.CHOOSEBIGCHANGE.COM/PAGES/BONUS25

Scan here

♡ Fun, fresh, transformational products + services: https://choosebigchange.com ♡

Wisdom Diaries

Dear Auntie,

I'm reaching out to you because I've been doing some deep soul-searching, and I could really use your guidance and wisdom. Specifically, I've been exploring ways to uncover uncomfortable archetypes within myself and heal deep emotional wounds that have been lingering beneath the surface for far too long.

I know that you have a deep understanding of the human psyche and a gift for helping others navigate the complexities of their inner worlds. I admire the way you approach life with courage and grace, and I believe that your insights can help me on this journey of self-discovery and healing.

I'm curious to know: How can I begin to uncover and explore the uncomfortable archetypes that reside within me? How can I shine a light on these shadowy aspects of myself with courage and compassion?

Once I've uncovered these archetypes, how can I begin the process of healing deep emotional wounds that may have been buried for years? It's a daunting task, to be sure, but it must be possible to heal even the deepest wounds and emerge stronger and more resilient than ever before.

I know that this work requires a great deal of courage and vulnerability, and I'm committed to approaching it with an open heart and a willingness to face whatever comes up. But I also know that I can't do it alone, and I'm grateful to have you by my side as a trusted confidante and guide.

I would love to hear your thoughts on how I can approach this work with courage and grace. What are some practices or techniques that you have found helpful in uncovering uncomfortable archetypes and healing deep emotional wounds? And how can I find support as I embark on this journey of self-discovery and healing?

Thank you for always being there for me and for sharing your wisdom and love so generously. I'm truly blessed to have you in my life.

> With love and gratitude,
> Your Niece

My Dearest Niece,

I received your letter with both gratitude and a deep sense of understanding. It takes immense courage to embark on the journey of uncovering uncomfortable archetypes and healing deep emotional wounds, and I commend you for your willingness to confront these aspects of yourself head-on.

You are absolutely right in recognizing that this work requires both courage and grace. It's a delicate balance of facing our shadows with compassion and vulnerability, while also holding space for ourselves to heal and grow. I'm honored that you would turn to me for guidance, and I'm more than happy to share some insights that I've gleaned from my own journey.

First and foremost, I want to encourage you to approach this work with gentleness and self-compassion. It's important to create a safe and supportive environment for yourself, free from judgment or self-criticism. Allow yourself to feel whatever emotions arise without pushing them away or trying to suppress them. Remember that healing is not a linear process, and it's okay to take things one step at a time.

One practice that I've found helpful in uncovering uncomfortable archetypes is journaling. Writing down your thoughts and feelings can help you gain clarity and insight into the patterns and beliefs that may be holding you back. Try to be as honest and raw as possible in your writing, and don't censor yourself or hold back.

In addition to journaling, mindfulness and meditation can also be powerful tools for exploring your inner landscape. Taking time each day to sit in stillness and observe your thoughts and emotions without judgment can help you develop a deeper understanding of yourself and the unconscious patterns that may be influencing your behavior.

When it comes to healing deep emotional wounds, I've found that self-compassion is key. Treat yourself with the same kindness and understanding that you would offer to a dear friend who is hurting. Allow yourself to grieve, to feel, and to process your emotions in whatever way feels right for you.

Lastly, remember that you don't have to go through this journey alone. Reach out to trusted friends, family members, or therapists who can offer support and guidance along the way. Healing is a collaborative process, and having a strong support system can make all the difference.

I believe in you and I have no doubt that you have the strength and resilience to navigate this journey with courage and grace. Remember to be gentle with yourself, to trust in the process, and to never underestimate the power of your own inner wisdom.

With all my love and support,
Your Auntie

♡ Fun, fresh, transformational products + services: https://choosebigchange.com ♡

Month End Review

◇ ◇ ◇

What was new, good, and different about this month?

_____
_____
_____
_____
_____
_____
_____
_____
_____
_____
_____
_____
_____
_____
_____
_____
_____
_____
_____
_____
_____
_____
_____

November

FEELING & HEALING

NOVEMBER 3–9

DO a review of your personal finances.
DO NOT act impulsively.

NOVEMBER 10–16

DO ctake an inventory of your leadership skills.
DO NOT fear your own individuality.

NOVEMBER 17–23

DO realize what you should let go of.
DO NOT be afraid to simply wherever possible.

NOVEMBER 24–30

DO realize it's okay to slow down.
DO NOT avoid a month-end review.

WHAT SPACE CAN I BE TO FEEL IT ALL AND HEAL IT ALL?

NOVEMBER 5, 8:19 AM

FULL MOON AT 13° TAURUS
ALLOWING CHANGES

NOVEMBER 20, 1:47 AM

NEW MOON AT 28° SCORPIO
AMPLIFIED INTUITION

Energy Almanac 2025 EDITION

Month At-A-Glance

◇◈◇

Write in the dates of this month before taking a few minutes to make notes of specific astrological time periods as they intersect with your own life happenings. You may even choose to highlight those time periods in green and red to remind yourself of easy and difficult days.

MONDAY	TUESDAY	WEDNESDAY	THURSDAY	FRIDAY	SATURDAY	SUNDAY

 Notes

November

◇◇◇

Things are cooling off outside and the once stunningly dressed trees are bare naked. But the heavens are dressed to the nines in 2025. One week has nothing but moons to handle and other weeks are packed to the brim with planetary movement. The first week of November is no exception. Generational planets Jupiter and Uranus are both moving retrograde imploring you to ask questions of yourself about your personal economy and self-worth as well as your emotional output. Spend some time with your journal deducing right answers. Mercury retrogrades in Scorpio on the 18th forcing you to look at your own transformation, too. Also mid-month is a grand trine in water signs encouraging more healing. It's the first of two water trines this month meant to harmonize healing. November 20 holds a beautiful sextile between the planet of revelation and the planet of imagination in the respective signs of Taurus and Pisces offering humanity a few days to enjoy a sense of spirituality as it relates to the economy. Later, when Venus enters Sagittarius on November 30 take an adventure with your partner to synthesize information and lessons learned. Your enthusiasm will be especially high.

By the way, if you're a planner, now is a great time to order the 2026 Energy Almanac. It's available at our website and on Amazon. Don't delay, grab yours now for holiday gift giving.

TRANSITS

11/2	**Daylight Saving Time ends**
11/3	**National Sandwich Day**
11/4	**Mars enters Sagittarius**
11/5	**Full Moon at 13° Taurus,** read moon article
11/6	**Venus enters Scorpio**
11/7	**Uranus Retrograde in Taurus**
11/9	**Mercury Retrograde in Sagittarius**
11/11	**Jupiter Retrograde in Cancer**
11/15	**Grand Trine in Water Signs: Jupiter, Sun, Saturn**
11/18	**Mercury Retrograde in Scorpio**
11/20	**Uranus in Taurus 29° sextile Neptune in Pisces 29°**
11/20	**New Moon at 28° Scorpio,** read moon article
11/21	**Sun enters Sagittarius, Happy birthday, Sagittarians!**

TRANSITS, CONT.

11/25	**Grand Trine in Water Signs: Jupiter, Venus, Saturn**
11/27	**Saturn direct in Pisces**
11/29	**Mercury direct in Scorpio**
11/30	**Venus enters Sagittarius**

RESOURCES

Numerology: 2 month in a 9 year

Gemstones: Amethyst, Turquoise

Oils: Helichrysum, Vetiver

Rituals: Expressive Arts Therapy, Healing Baths or Showers, Movement For Emotional Release

Wisdom Diaries: Cultivating Self-Compassion

ORACLE PLAY

"What do I need to know about the month ahead?"

CARD 1	CARD 2	CARD 3	CARD 4	CARD 5

_____

_____

_____

_____

♡ Fun, fresh, transformational products + services: https://choosebigchange.com ♡

NOVEMBER PREDICTIONS

MONDAY, NOVEMBER 3 – SUNDAY, NOVEMBER 9	**MOONS:** ARIES, TAURUS, GEMINI

This week Mars, planet of action, enters Sagittarius for a five week visit just in time for the holidays. It seems you may feel the urge to be on the move, adventuring, and perhaps learning even more about what you believe. Studying higher philosophies is part of Sagittarian living. Also on Monday is National Sandwich Day. This calls for great bread and delightful fillings that only you can decide. Be sure to take a picture of that meal and tag us on social media. On Wednesday morning the Full Moon in Taurus will awaken you to something you can release. Perhaps it's quite personal, like undervaluing yourself? Whatever it is, let it go. Read about this lunation and do your own releasing ritual. Our article is on page 160. Following the new moon Venus makes a shift. Wearing the zodiac of Scorpio Venus becomes passionate about transformation. Take note that the urge to morph relationships is there and a change in joint finances could be on the table, too.

The last transit of the week is on Friday when the planet of revelation goes retrograde. Uranus retrograde in Taurus is the opportunity for society to look at the recent changes in the economy. Uranus is futuristic, digital, and insightful while Taurus is traditional. It's been a long battle between the old and the new and this retrograde is the opportunity to assimilate information and questions. "How are any new monetary systems working for the collective?" and "What adjustments still need to be made with the economy?" Don't be afraid to look at your personal finances as well under this influence. You have through February 2026 to do so.

Sunday Mercury slows his roll and goes retrograde in the sign of Sagittarius and now you should slow your roll, too. Understand that examining the right use of your language is the right use of Mercury retrograde in Sagittarius. Watch communication and travel carefully. You might want to stay closer to home.

GIFT & SHADOW THIS WEEK: *The North (destiny) and South Nodes (karma) shift again this week into Gate 63-Doubt and Gate 64-Confusion. Both Gates sit on the Head Center in your Human Design, the center for ideas and inspiration. The shadow of these two Gates becomes apparent when we overly rely on our minds to answer questions like how and why. The Gate 64 creates confusion when we are hurrying to discover "how" something is meant to happen. We learn with this Gate to relax and allow the epiphany or revelation to occur. The South Node in the Gate of Doubt represents the need for us to be discerning about what information we are taking in and then acting upon. We tend to leap into and out of things quickly now. Instead, slow down and allow your intuition or emotions to align with a decision before you act impulsively.*

GRAB THE 2026 ENERGY ALMANAC. NOW AVAILABLE AT:
WWW.CHOOSEBIGCHANGE.COM

Grab
Yours

MONDAY, NOVEMBER 10 – SUNDAY, NOVEMBER 16

MOONS: CANCER, LEO, VIRGO, LIBRA

How interesting is it that November 11 (11/11) hosts the start of Jupiter retrograde in Cancer and we collectively reflect on the emotional output and nurturing of each other? This time period is an opportunity to observe and make note of the rights and wrongs of recent months. Ask big questions and get big answers. "Has my emotionality been justified or just over-the-top? How can I use my intuition to serve the greater good? What is a high use of my nurturing skills?" The rest of the week is moon oriented with transits in Cancer, Leo, Virgo and Libra. Use your notebook to continue your learning about how you respond to these zodiac signs. Are you more playful under Leo influences and more practical and orderly with Virgo? Pay close attention, this is information for the ages. Also leaving an imprint on the ages is Saturday's Grand Trine in water signs creating what could be an emotional weekend. Jupiter in Cancer, the Sun in Scorpio, and Saturn retrograde in Pisces will tug our heart strings and bring us closer to healing. Order more tissues on Monday the tenth, just in case. While you're ordering that you might want to pick up the next Energy Almanac, too. It's available as a paperback or ebook.

GIFT & SHADOW THIS WEEK: *The planet Uranus moves back into Gate 8-Contribution this week. As the planet of awakening, Uranus tends to create situations where we must seek to express our authenticity. In Gate 8, we tend to shut down our individuality in favor of "fitting in," which means we are all not quite sure who we are. The result is that from now through the end of 2025, we might struggle to identify and take action on our personal dreams. The struggle will encourage us to break out of and break through any barriers to being our true selves. Inside, every person is a genius—your job is to find yours and live it out loud!*

_____

_____

♡ Fun, fresh, transformational products + services: https://choosebigchange.com ♡

MONDAY, NOVEMBER 17 – SUNDAY, NOVEMBER 23

It's a big week Little Pretzel. It's as though the cosmos forgot that there's a Thanksgiving Dinner to prepare. Let's start with Mercury already retrograde, changing signs. Tuesday he enters Scorpio. Here you have the opportunity to analyze your own transformation. Applying logical thinking to something as enigmatic as personal change can be a challenge, but one worth taking. Standard mercurial topics apply as well like potential communication issues becoming confused and technology corrupting itself. The retrograde lasts through December first.

Thursday presents you with Uranus (revelation) in Taurus (the economy) stimulating Neptune (imagination) in Pisces at the karmic 29th degree. Little Pretzel, this is one for the books as not only is this transit present but it is on the same day as the New Moon in Scorpio, more about the moon itself on page 160. Expect the unexpected for a day or two. If you didn't highlight these days in your calendar earlier in the month perhaps highlight your calendar now. Uranus and Neptune are both preparing to leave their current zodiac outfits and slip into new ones early in 2026. Imagine two dancers, one in a space suit and one in an artist's smock. As they tango a moment happens when they come nose to nose in an intense pose. They are holding hands, chest to chest and the music is pounding behind them. They are flirting! The two will bring out the best of one another and because they are at the special 29th degree the events of the day will ring forward into the future, flavoring it with potentials. Will spirituality (Neptune/Pisces) finally make its way into the changing economy (Uranus/Taurus)? Will we get sudden insights (Uranus/Taurus) that create a grand vision for new uses with money? The possibilities are fun to play with. As part of your continued learning make a list of the two planets and their descriptors and the two zodiacs and their descriptors. Mix and match phrases to come up with some surprise endings. From Janet Hickox of Living-Astrology.com, "One big phrase comes to mind—Spiritual Awakening! A time of inventiveness and innovation and also a period where we are more insightful and open to our intuition."

Sunday the Sun enters Sagittarius. Note that your own sense of adventure and routine are present now through mid-December.

GIFT & SHADOW THIS WEEK: *We might call this week's gift the art of simplification, while the shadow could be named the disaster of complexity! In reality, we have built a civilization and our lives on very complex ideas, schedules, and patterns. Isn't it time to pare them down and live more simply? Take a look at your life this week from the perspective of complexity. What might you be able to let go of? Are all those unworn shoes in your closet just clogging up the space? If so, simply give some of them away.*

✻ Get your book bonus offers: www.choosebigchange.com/pages/bonus25 ✻

MONDAY, NOVEMBER 24 – SUNDAY, NOVEMBER 30

MOONS: CAPRICORN, AQUARIUS, PISCES

Following the hullabaloo of last week we have a joyously healing week to lean into. Of note is Tuesday's Grand Trine in...say it with me...water signs. It seems 2025 has an important theme of healing and this trine delivers, as the others did, an opportunity to feel the joy and pain, the delight and the despair and trust that everything will right itself. Let your heart burst open, really Rumi-style, remember "the wound is the place where the light enters you."After your monthly review and goal setting session, if you need some additional homework this week, research Rumi and get lost in the sweetness of his ancient wisdom. Sunday's Pisces moon seems perfect for that job.

GIFT & SHADOW THIS WEEK: *Sometimes life can get hectic, especially around the holidays. We find ourselves running around trying to get things done or jumping from one thing to another, multi-tasking, as it were. Well, that energy can become amplified this week as the Sun in Gate 34-Power gives us the energy and power to get a lot done. Just because we "could" get a lot done doesn't mean we should take on more than usual. This is one of the Gates in Human Design that can lead to burnout—especially for the Projectors, Manifestors, and Reflectors. Slow down, take a deep breath, and prioritize what action to take.*

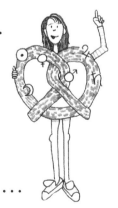

STAY IN ALIGNMENT WITH THE PLANETS! FIND INSPIRED JEWELRY, LOVE & LIGHT APPAREL, MUGS, ART PRINTS AND MORE :

WWW.CHOOSEBIGCHANGE.COM

♡ Fun, fresh, transformational products + services: https://choosebigchange.com ♡

November Moon Work

NOVEMBER 5, 8:19 AM FULL MOON AT 13° TAURUS		**ALLOWING CHANGES**

The November full moon may find you wrestling with your own transformation. The sun in Taurus prefers stability while the moon is full of mystery and magnetism and it's calling you to look at your individuality. Will you stand firm or make your way into a new version of yourself? Your mind is actively seeking answers as well as adventures thanks to Mercury and Mars both in Sagittarius, but you won't be able to escape the multitude of questions that are bubbling to the surface through Uranus' retrograde. Your faith is part of the equation and that leadership topic is always present, too. We've said it month after month in this year's almanac. What kind of leader will you be? This is the year to develop your vision of that and then build it out over the next few years.

As partnerships go you may note strain. Venus is aspected by Jupiter, Pluto, and Chiron. Your emotions could surely be high as you work on sorting through the world's transformation.

The big guns Jupiter, Saturn, and Neptune are in a harmonious trine encouraging big use of intuition and imagination as you build your leadership legs. This is a subtle wave playing out in your unconscious mind.

If there is confusion (Neptune) or pressure (Saturn) weighing on you be sure to do some journaling for clarity and practical next steps to help unravel the mystery.

AFFIRMATION: *"I am actively shifting and engaged in my own change."*

MOON WORK:

- Earthy Taurus energy loves his/her nest and food and pretty things. Plan a beautiful farm-to-table meal at home. Raise a glass to this month's intentions for creating change in spite of any resistance.
- Try using emotional freedom technique tapping on the topic of resistance so that you are more able to take steps toward shifting. Try the "EFT For Resistance" video on YouTube at this channel: @TamIAmV
- Map out your leadership goals. Even if you are only leading your family or a group of friends, there is always room for development. What do you need to adjust to improve yourself? Brainstorm ideas and then put them into action.

_____

_____

_____

_____

_____

_____

_____

_____

NOVEMBER 20, 1:47 AM
NEW MOON AT 28° SCORPIO

AMPLIFIED INTUITION

If you're feeling temperamental or intense today, you must look at the sun, moon, and Mercury all in the penetrating sign of Scorpio. These three are all being triggered and amplified by both Jupiter, Saturn, and Neptune. This is bringing incredible intuition to the fore. If ever you wanted answers, this would be the time to ask, and listen. Stay mindful that Neptune's presence in the sign of Aries could intensify the passion or create confusion. If spirituality is at the front of your mind then know that impassioned action (Neptune in Aries) is likely, especially if it will benefit humanitarian efforts (Pluto in Aquarius).

Venus and Mars are tangling with the north node in Aries. One is ready to tango and the other is Mars is ready to tackle. North node is the collective sacred wound we are trying to heal. Each individual works their own personal experiences to edge their way to healing the hurt around confidence, individuality, and having courage to lead. This is an ongoing theme through your moon work for all of 2025. By this point in the year, you aren't the same person who opened this book in January. You've molted, and there is still more work to do.

Jupiter, now retrograde in the fuzzy pink housecoat of Cancer, is trine Saturn and Neptune also retrograde. Neptune and Saturn are in the flowing artist's smock of Pisces. These three are amiable and pulling you inward hoping you will listen to the whispers of the cosmos. The topic of conversation between the three is big and covers compassion, faith, spirituality and right use of your visualization powers and personal clairvoyance.

This moon above all others is zesty! Black Moon Lilith is another cosmic aspect who is highly in play today. This luminary represents rebellion, sexuality and the more primal feminine aspects of life. Note that she is being triggered by seven celestial bodies. If sensuality is top of mind or if you are feeling a little lawless, it's okay. Your dark side is showing and that's perfectly correct under the darkness of the New Moon. Set your intentions to uncover what may be holding back your own transformation. That's a mystery worth solving!

AFFIRMATION: *"I am unmasking the mysteries of my life, my passion serves me well."*

MOON WORK:

- This moon offers many, many opportunities to receive messages from source. Your instincts will be sharp. Capture all of it in a journal.
- Research Black Moon Lilith to better understand how this celestial body works to show you your own "taboo" potentials. Once you understand her, find her placement in your own natal birth chart.
- Just for fun, dress mysteriously by wearing black all day. See how it makes you feel. Journal the results.

_____

_____

_____

_____

_____

_____

♡ Fun, fresh, transformational products + services: https://choosebigchange.com ♡

Numerology

Numerologically this is a two month in a nine year.
November = 11 and 2025 = 9; 11 + 9 = 20; 2 + 0 = 2

Two energy brings harmony. This feminine energy includes diplomacy and strength which partners well with the wisdom of the nine. Tap into these helpful forces in November as you work through some deep healing.

Gemstones & Oils

GEMSTONES

Amethyst Connected to the violet flame—divine source, it enhances spirituality, psychic abilities, and contentment. Amethyst stimulates the third eye and crown chakra. It purifies the aura of any toxins or negativity, and encourages sobriety, self love, and self control.

Turquoise Invites serenity, refreshes the mind, clears old thought processes, aids in smooth communication, boosts clairaudience and clairvoyance, and promotes balanced friendships.

OILS

Helichrysum *Helichrysum italicum*
Sacred healer, detoxifying, compassion
Blends well w/ Lavender, Geranium, Lemon, Tea Tree

Everlasting, aka Helichrysum, works a lot like chamomile, encouraging both deep seeded psychological and physical wounds to heal. Everlasting is a pungent intense aroma. It is a reminder that this oil is beneficial for those deep challenging wounds we have been living with for years. Through purification/cleansing of the organs, Helichrysum has the power to remove intense wounds and promote healthy change.

Vetiver *Vetiveria zizanoides*
Emotional grounding, release, restoring, trauma transforming
Blends well w/ Orange, Patchouli, Geranium, Rose

Vetiver's deep earthy notes sends us deep into the muck of our emotions and feelings. Finding the root of your healing challenges, bathing you in warm nourishing soil, she revitalizes your root chakra enabling you to better interpret and handle darker wounds, particularly those of ancestral energies or genetic inheritances or childhood trauma. Vetiver says "You're safe, slow down, breathe, take it all in." Watch how your perspective of your negative experiences changes and see how you now view the dirt and muck as shiny glittering stars of your future.

_____

_____

Rhythms, Routines & Rituals

Ever feel like your emotions are playing hide and seek, and you're the one left searching blindfolded? That's where the magic of these rituals help you release the energies of November like a champ.

- **Expressive Arts Therapy:** Tap into your inner child. Play with expressive arts, such as drawing, painting, or writing, to explore and express your emotions. Even if it's simply getting out the old crayons, use creativity as a tool for emotional release. I bought some fingerpaints to get messy and expressive.

- **Healing Baths or Showers:** Get wet! Water is incredibly soothing and healing. Add some healing elements into your baths or showers, such as calming scents or soothing music. I can make a bath an event. Bring on the bath bombs and bubbles!

- **Movement For Emotional Release:** Get your groove on. Engage in physical activities like dance, yoga, or tai chi as a form of emotional release. Moving your body moves energy. Whether it's overwhelm, sadness or anger, start by shaking it off. My motto is that it's always the right time for a dance party!

Of course, if you find that your emotional challenges are overwhelming, consider seeking professional support from a therapist or counselor. You got this! To create more nurturing routines, grab my bonus material.

_____
_____
_____
_____
_____
_____
_____
_____
_____

GRAB THE 2026 ENERGY ALMANAC. NOW AVAILABLE AT:
WWW.CHOOSEBIGCHANGE.COM

♡ Fun, fresh, transformational products + services: https://choosebigchange.com ♡

Wisdom Diaries

Dear Dad,

I hope this letter finds you well. I've been doing some soul-searching lately, prompted by the craziness in the world these days, and I wanted to reach out to you for guidance. I've been contemplating the importance of emotional healing, and creating a safe space for myself to explore my full range of emotions. I was hoping you could share some techniques or tips for fostering a non-judgmental and accepting internal environment.

Growing up, I've always admired how you've been able to hold space for me and allow me to express myself freely, without fear of judgment or criticism. I've come to realize that having a safe space to explore my emotions is crucial for my emotional well-being, and I want to learn how to create that for myself as I continue to navigate life's ups and downs.

I'm curious to know: What are some techniques or practices that you've found helpful for cultivating non-judgment and acceptance, both for yourself and for others? How do you create a safe space within yourself where you can fully experience and process your emotions without feeling ashamed or guilty?

Additionally, I've been thinking a lot about the concept of being a friend to myself. I know that self-compassion and self-love are essential for my mental and emotional health, but I sometimes struggle with being kind and gentle with myself, especially during difficult times. How do you practice being a friend to yourself, and what wisdom can you offer me as I strive to cultivate more compassion and love for myself?

I know these are big questions, but I trust your wisdom and experience, Dad. Your guidance has always meant the world to me, and I'm grateful to have you as my mentor and role model as I continue to grow and evolve on this journey of self-discovery.

Thank you for always being there for me and for your unwavering love and support. I look forward to hearing your thoughts and insights.

> With love and gratitude,
> Your Child

Hey There,

Your letter touched me deeply, and I want you to know that I am here for you, always, ready to offer whatever guidance and support you may need. Your willingness to explore your emotions and cultivate self-compassion is a testament to your strength and maturity, and I couldn't be prouder of the person you've become.

Creating a safe space for yourself to explore your emotions is a journey, and it's one that I'm honored to walk alongside you. One technique that I've found helpful for fostering non-judgment and acceptance is mindfulness. By practicing mindfulness, you can learn to observe your thoughts and emotions without getting caught up in them or judging them as good or bad. Simply allowing yourself to experience whatever arises with curiosity and compassion can create a profound sense of spaciousness and acceptance within yourself.

Another important aspect of creating a safe space for yourself is setting boundaries with others. It's okay to communicate your needs and boundaries clearly and assertively, and to surround yourself with people who respect and support you unconditionally. Remember that you deserve to be treated with kindness and respect, and don't be afraid to advocate for yourself and your emotional well-being.

As for being a friend to yourself, I've found that self-compassion is the key. Treat yourself with the same kindness, understanding, and compassion that you would offer to a dear friend who is struggling. Be gentle with yourself during difficult times, and remind yourself that you are worthy of love and acceptance just as you are, flaws and all.

Lastly, remember that self-compassion is a skillset that takes time to develop. It's okay to stumble along the way, just remember to be patient and forgiving with yourself as you learn and grow. Trust in yourself and your ability to navigate life's challenges with grace and resilience, and know that I am here to support you every step of the way.

> With all my love and admiration,
> Your Dad

✻ Get your book bonus offers: www.choosebigchange.com/pages/bonus25 ✻

Month End Review

◇·◇·◇

What was new, good, and different about this month?

_____

_____

_____

_____

_____

_____

_____

_____

_____

_____

_____

_____

_____

_____

_____

_____

_____

_____

_____

_____

_____

_____

Energy Almanac 2025 Edition

December

THE BUSINESS OF THE SOUL

DECEMBER 1-7

DO plan time for nesting this week.
DO NOT get carried away by enthusiasm.

DECEMBER 8-14

DO order your Energy Almanac for the year ahead.
DO NOT be aggressive about sharing your opinions.

DECEMBER 15-21

DO embody more and more love.
DO NOT avoid planning for next year.

DECEMBER 22-28

DO renegotiate where needed.
DO NOT stay in one-sided agreements.

DECEMBER 29-31

DO plan a creative New Year's party.
DO NOT avoid a year-end review.

HOW EASY CAN IT BE TO BE SEEN AS AN INTUITIVE AND HEART-CENTERED LEADER?

DECEMBER 4, 6:14 PM

FULL MOON AT 13° GEMINI
A CURIOUS MIND

DECEMBER 19, 8:43 PM

NEW MOON AT 28° SAGITTARIUS
NEW POINT OF VIEW

Energy Almanac 2025 edition

Month At-A-Glance

◇◇◇

Write in the dates of this month before taking a few minutes to make notes of specific astrological time periods as they intersect with your own life happenings. You may even choose to highlight those time periods in green and red to remind yourself of easy and difficult days.

MONDAY	TUESDAY	WEDNESDAY	THURSDAY	FRIDAY	SATURDAY	SUNDAY

Notes

December

—◇◇◇—

With mittens and gloves covering your hands, you can applaud the planets for finally allowing you a chance to catch your breath. Not void of transits, but not packed to the brim as October and November were, you can use these 31 days for handling holiday tasks. The Full Moon falls in the first week of the month and the second week has our thoughts speeding along in the social sign of Sagittarius when Mercury stations direct. There is an edge of "all business" to the bulk of December as Mars, the sun, and Venus all wear the three-piece suit of Capricorn. Seriousness, goal-setting, and disciplined task tending will help to fuel your days as you wrap, cook, and socialize. The biggest transit to watch for is the December 21 square between Jupiter, planet of expansion, and Chiron, the collective wound. It seems one is pulling for use of intuitive information and strong emotion while the other one may be afraid to be seen as a soulful leader. Don't let the planets cool you. Wrap up 2025 with plenty of routine journaling so you can capture the good efforts you've made again this month while making note of what can be adjusted in the new year.

TRANSITS

12/4	**Full Moon at 13° Gemini,** read moon article
12/10	**Neptune direct in Pisces**
12/11	**Mercury stations direct in Sagittarius**
12/12	**Gingerbread House Day**
12/15	**Mars enters Capricorn**
12/19	**New Moon at 28° Sagittarius,** read moon article
12/21	**Sun enters Capricorn.** **Happy birthday, Capricorns!**
12/21	**Winter Solstice**
12/24	**Venus enters Capricorn**

RESOURCES

Numerology: 3 month in a 9 year

Gemstones: Amber, Labradorite

Oils: Marjoram, Rosemary

Rituals: Year-End Reflection Ritual, Seek Feedback

Wisdom Diaries: Leading with Love

ORACLE PLAY

"What do I need to know about the month ahead?"

CARD 1   CARD 2   CARD 3   CARD 4   CARD 5

_____

_____

_____

_____

♡ Fun, fresh, transformational products + services: https://choosebigchange.com ♡

DECEMBER PREDICTIONS

MONDAY, DECEMBER 1 – SUNDAY, DECEMBER 7   MOONS: ARIES, TAURUS, GEMINI, CANCER

Your goal for the month is set and Monday you can initiate! Aries influences will spur you toward action—use the Taurus energy for holiday shopping on Tuesday if you'd like. A great gift for those spiritually minded like you, is the Energy Almanac for 2026. The real action happens on Thursday with the social Gemini Full Moon. Known for their wit and intelligence, this moon could find you sharp as a tack as you hunt down anything in the way of your ambitions. Read more on page 173 of this publication. The weekend is meant for nesting. Maybe pull out your decorations and for nostalgia's sake, write a story of the history of the more meaningful pieces of decor that you own. Some lucky recipient of the ornament will thank you later.

GIFT & SHADOW THIS WEEK: *The Sun is in Gate 9-Focus, and the Earth is in Gate 16-Enthusiasm this week. As we move toward the holiday season, this week is an optimal time to determine the level of focus and concentration, or lack thereof, in your life. This week offers the opportunity to tune into what is most important to you, for example, your passion, and keep your focus in a manageable amount of areas. We have enthusiasm and a zest for life on board this week, which is fantastic! But we can get carried away with enthusiasm and lose focus. Fragmentation results in that feeling of ADD or ADHD when we are trying to focus on too many things (and likely not essential things). Restore your mind by choosing what is most important and turning your focus there.*

_____

_____

MONDAY, DECEMBER 8 – SUNDAY, DECEMBER 14   MOONS: LEO, VIRGO, LIBRA

2025 has had some seriously spiritual moments in it. It's lucky that this week we get to take it emotionally easy. Mercury will station direct mid-week and you should remain on high alert as to how you share information and opinions. Fire-hosing friends and family members with your own version of truth can be off-putting. Best to "bite thy tongue" and instead channel high spirits toward optimistic outlooks and expansive visions of happy times ahead. Friday employs Virgo energy for service to others and practical work routines. How might you volunteer? It is the holiday season, and lucky enough Friday is also Gingerbread House Day. Put those Virgo hands to work building something tasty and beautiful. The weekend is impacted with Libra energy which means partnerships and peace keeping are highlighted. Don't forget to order your Energy Almanac for next year.

GIFT & SHADOW THIS WEEK: *We can explore the art of integrity this week with the Sun in Gate 26-Integrity. And really, it is an art. We all seem to have a definition of integrity that is strictly moralistic and is dictated to us by society. However, other forms of integrity are very important, too. For example, integrity to self or being true to your purpose. Integrity really is in the eyes of the beholder. Your truth is yours and cannot be downloaded to others. Align yourself to your truth and values, and integrity becomes easy. Another critical theme with Earth in Gate 45-Distribution this week is monetary and concerns sharing of wealth. Generosity and kindness are rewarded as a way to keep abundance flowing.*

_____

_____

MONDAY, DECEMBER 15 – SUNDAY, DECEMBER 21   **MOONS:** LIBRA, SCORPIO, SAGITTARIUS

When Mars enters Capricorn early this week, you can expect a solid foundation to be put under your world. You'll have Monday through late January to start planning tasks and setting goals. It's serious business that you'll have the impetus to work on. Friday brings the ever-lively New Moon in Sagittarius which could have you feeling boisterous. Pull on your rose colored glasses and set a higher-than-normal vision for the next moon cycle. Read more about this lunation on page 174. The week wraps up on Sunday with the sun's move into Capricorn. Happy birthday to the sea-goat who can maneuver both water and mountains and attain what they set their sights on. Notice a more serious attitude in yourself and if you haven't already, it's time to buy a planner that prepares you for the year ahead. Also on Sunday is a square between Jupiter in Cancer and Chiron in Aries. Remember, Chiron represents our collective soul wound, currently represented by the star athlete Aries. Will your emotions bump against actions you need to take? Will your desire to stay home and nest create high emotion because there are things that need to get done? Is your intuition telling you something you didn't want to hear? Squares force movement and something is sure to give. As a reminder, and as we have said before, keep calm and Aries on; your leadership style is all developing perfectly.

GIFT & SHADOW THIS WEEK: *We are again at the turning of the seasons, which allows us to embody more and more love into our lives. This time, the Sun in Gate 10 Self-love and Earth in Gate 15-Compassion for our fellow human beings are in focus. In these energies' lower expression or shadow, we forget how loveable, worthy, and valuable we all are. Do a self-love inventory. Have you been making decisions in favor of you or against you? When it comes to loving compassion for your fellow humans, are you turning a blind eye to the plight of those less fortunate, or do you pitch in and help where you can? Acts of love are favored this week.*

MONDAY, DECEMBER 22 – SUNDAY, DECEMBER 28   **MOONS:** CAPRICORN, AQUARIUS, PISCES

It is Christmas week and all is well with only moon influences to mind along with some informational content for your notebook. While Monday is all business, probably prepping for the big day, on Wednesday Venus, ruler of love and money, enters Capricorn making it the third luminary in this business-suit zodiac. With both Mars and now Venus here you have some semblance of balance. The right and left brain are simpatico when it comes to bringing order, getting things done, and laying a foundation. Venus will temper the urge to constantly work. Loyalty is at a high point, and goal-getting is weighty, too. It seems perfectly timed that this influence will be strong as we wrap up 2025 and saunter sideways into 2026. Planning and patience when mapping out your strategies is a fortunate influence.

There is still time to get your Energy Almanac before the year ends. It's available as a paperback and as a digital download. Get yours at: www.ChooseBigChange.com.

GIFT & SHADOW THIS WEEK: *The North and South Nodes shift again this week. The North Node, or destiny, moves into Gate 37-Peace, and the South Node, karma, moves into Gate 40-Restoration. Consider how peace, or its absence, plays a role in your relationships. These two Gates actually form the Channel of Community in your Human Design, and we have an opportunity to rewrite or renegotiate our agreements with everyone in our lives. If the agreements you have been involved with are one-sided or create win-lose situations for you, now is the time to make them win-win!*

MONDAY, DECEMBER 29 – SUNDAY, JANUARY 4

MOONS: ARIES, TAURUS, GEMINI

Three, two, one day left in 2025 and Little Pretzel, you should be proud. Monday's influence is the moon in Aries and boldness is encouraged. Tuesday is the moon in Taurus, offering you the chance to take one final look at your personal self-worth and your home budget. When that work is done, go to the store and grab yourself a gorgeous potted herbal plant. Tauruses love Mother Earth. Have some live plants nearby as you close out this year. If you choose herbs, you win twice by both enjoying growing them as well as eating them. Triple win! They are medicinal, too. The final day of 2025 is made for nesting. Cozy up to a hot meal, warm drinks, and cool conversation with family and friends. Get creative on New Year's Eve. Make your own pasta, do crafts or collage, anything that is tactile is appropriate.

As you wind down 2025, give thanks for a year of wisdom, closure, and your own enlightenment. It's been one for the books. Thank you, Little Pretzel, for letting the Energy Almanac into your world. You are deeply appreciated.

For information about where Mercury is going on Thursday, open your 2026 Energy Almanac and smile. Your planning just became even more powerful. Don't have yours yet? Go to: www.ChooseBigChange.com for a paperback or digital ebook. And download the new bonuses for the year ahead.

GIFT & SHADOW THIS WEEK: *The Sun is at Gate 58-Joy, and the Earth at Gate 52-Stillness this week. We can struggle with joy and peace during Christmas week. It's such a hectic time for most people, and then for others, there is an absence perhaps of family and festivities. Joy is an inside job as it does not originate outside of as we think it does. Instead, it comes as an alignment to what makes us happy. Your alignment with happiness (and peace) exudes to others in your world. We cannot make others happy or give others joy, but we can certainly set the stage for them to experience it for themselves. Your actions have an impact, but so do your attitudes. Let your Joy and Peace be as breath to you.*

December Moon Work

DECEMBER 4, 6:14 PM		A CURIOUS MIND
FULL MOON AT 13° GEMINI	○	

While the Sun, Venus, and Mars are all wearing a t-shirt and backpack as all adventuresome Sagittarians do, there could be a strong urge to travel. These three planets are tense against the North Node which adds a bit of strain to the typical Sag chumminess. You may require a dose of bravery in order to handle any plans you've made and the Moon in Gemini is opposing all the aforementioned planets which may force a complete rain date. You'll really feel the resistance between play or being a party pooper.

Your language could be tainted with harshness as you receive information and potentially spew it out too fast. Be sure to manage your tongue for a few days. Mercury in Scorpio is trine Jupiter in Cancer and Saturn in Pisces.

As societal and generational planets pick, poke, and prod one another tonight, you should simply stay alert to the ongoing topics at hand: global transformation of groups of people, innovation, technology, the economy and world leaders. When we say world leaders, we include you in that! These planets are working on everyone to make a case for growth. Each individual evolution adds to the warp and weft of the fabric of this world. Make note of the urges you feel pulled toward and discover tonight what's in the way of your own contribution.

If this moon has you intuiting about a social night on the town, it's okay. Don't hesitate—go, have fun! Often, experiences on the town can lead to interesting growth points, which is what the North Nodes wants from you anyway.

AFFIRMATION: *"I am willing to grow beyond what I already know."*

MOON WORK:
- Geminis are social beings and curious, too! How can you make this night social and educational at the same time?
- Research a topic you're interested in. Gemini is the sign of exploration. If you can't go out, this would be a good use of your time.
- Meditate once again on the global landscape. Imagine a world where peace and plenty are the norm. Your visualization is perfectly timed and contributes in immeasurable ways.

Hope reigns supreme and adventure (or philosophizing) awaits under the December 4 Full Moon in the gregarious and altruistic sign of the archer. The sun and moon are hip to hip with Venus, also in Sagittarius, and Mars in Capricorn. Here you have the business of adventure and philosophy—what a great day that makes. But wait! Saturn is wanting you to push the boundaries of your spirituality and Neptune is working on that theme, too. Should you really hold the beliefs you've held for so long or is there a growth point tonight that could close the year on a high note? Your active and futuristic mind (Mercury in Sagittarius) is dwelling on leadership topics again. It's a philosophical conundrum as to whether you should hold tight to your current thoughts or create space for new ones.

If you've been feeling larger than life, that's Venus whispering to you. Today she is urging you toward stepping up and imagining yourself in a stronger position. Her friend Mars is serious about setting a strong foundation in your life. He's ready to build things but again Neptune nudges toward more faith and compassion. His presence confuses the mind. Let the steam settle and just lean toward love

Ask questions and listen for intuitive answers. This never ending theme in 2025 is just that—never ending. We are urged to live instinctively. We are being encouraged to use our inner compass to make decisions about every aspect of our lives. As we become more conscious, we can hear the whispers of the cosmos. Jupiter, Saturn, Neptune and Uranus are all influencing our inner eyes and ears—our sixth senses. Our jobs are to apply that to our own lives first and then to trust that it will ripple out into society.

Feel hopeful under the Sagittarian moon, in spite of all the inner conflict that may be going on. Set your intentions toward new belief systems, new points of view, roads as yet untraveled, and breaking routines that have you in a stranglehold.

AFFIRMATION: *"I am actively listening to my intuition and am willing to lean into new ways of thinking."*

MOON WORK:

- Sagittarians do enjoy travel but also can get stuck in routine patterns. Use this moon to identify old beliefs that may no longer be true for you and what routine thinking you could let fall away.
- Watch your words. In fact, grab your journal and pull out the pages that have negative self-talk or judgmental words in them and burn them ceremonially. Make a pact with yourself to speak kindly or don't speak at all.
- Grab a book on a new theological topic. Choose something you wouldn't normally step toward. This will expand your horizons and bring you on a new kind of adventure.

_____

_____

_____

_____

_____

_____

Numerology

Numerologically this is a three month in a nine year.
December = 12 and 2025 = 9; 12 + 9 = 21; 2 + 1 = 3

The final month of the year carries the creative energy of the 3. Communication will be high and playful and when merged with the wisdom of the 9 your advice may be more easily received than ever.

Gemstones & Oils

GEMSTONES

Amber Brightens the soul and solar plexus, lifts the spirit and heals the body. Brings forth the energies of Mother Earth. Amber offers you patience, protection, psychic shielding, loyalty, sensuality, nurturing, and healing.

Labradorite Increases determination, focus, and attention, it shields and repairs the aura, activates the third eye, raises consciousness and heightens intuition, enhances dream recall, willpower, and compassion. Banishes stress, fear and insecurities.

OILS

Marjoram *Origanum majorana*
Comfort, self-love
Blends well w/ Rose, Bergamot, Peppermint, Eucalyptus

Marjoram, the herb of love, joy of the mountains, warms the heart and mind, like a warm embrace from a loved one or in the way the sun warms the icy cold mountains as she rises. It drives us inward, yearning to nest within ourselves, drawing the homebody out of us. Marjoram encourages rest, self love, and compassion. It's a beautiful oil to diffuse while you snuggle at home on the couch, refilling your heart with contentment.

Rosemary *Rosmarinus officinalis*
Destiny, future clarity, planning
Blends well w/ Black Pepper, Bergamot, Lavender, Fir, Marjoram

Rosemary has an innate ability to quickly tone, stimulate and clarify the thoughts of the mind. With such clarity, Rosemary draws the potential of the future and brings new inspiration and a new outlook on life. It will stimulate you to declutter your mind, your house, your office and harness determination to make changes for a healthy ego, avoiding all the doom and gloom of a poor sense of worth.

_____

_____

_____

♡ Fun, fresh, transformational products + services: https://choosebigchange.com ♡

Rhythms, Routines & Rituals

We've explored rituals and routines throughout the year to create a bridge between the physical and the spiritual, offering a space for personal growth and transformation. This month's practices and tools allow us to recalibrate, develop a deeper understanding of ourselves and our journey this year, and prepare us to move forward.

- **Engage in a Year-End Reflection Ritual:** Wrap up the year with a chill year-end check-in. Look back, high-five yourself for the wins, and jot down where you can level up. Brew a cup of tea or pop a bottle of champagne and celebrate your journey.

- **Seek Feedback:** Whether it's with your team at work, your family or your partner, tune in to make sure everyone's on the same wavelength, making things better together. On our anniversary every year, my husband and I have a "state of the union" conversation. It's important to acknowledge where we've been, and where we're going.

When we vibe with our body, heart, and life's rhythm, it's like hitting pause on the chaos. No more running in circles, just finding our groove throughout the year. Knowing our energy flow and crafting routines to ride that wave lets us live in alignment and flow—peak productivity when we're on fire, and hardcore self-love during chill moments. It's not too late to grab my bonus material and reuse it for the year ahead. Get it now before it's gone.

_____

_____

_____

_____

_____

_____

_____

_____

_____

_____

_____

GRAB THE 2026 ENERGY ALMANAC. NOW AVAILABLE AT:
WWW.CHOOSEBIGCHANGE.COM

Grab Yours

Dear Me,

Today, I want to pose a question, one that I believe holds the potential to unlock new insights and possibilities in life. How easy can it be to be seen as an intuitive and heart-centered leader?

Take a moment to sit with that question, allowing it to sink into the depths of your being. Consider what it means to you to embody the qualities of intuition and heart-centered leadership. Imagine yourself stepping into that role with confidence and authenticity, guiding others with wisdom and compassion.

Now, I want you to challenge any preconceived notions or limiting beliefs that may arise in response to this question. How often do you find yourself doubting your own intuition or holding back from expressing your true heart-centered nature? What fears or insecurities are holding you back from fully embracing your potential as a leader?

Remember, being seen as an intuitive and heart-centered leader doesn't mean having all the answers or being perfect. It's about trusting your instincts, listening to your inner guidance, and showing up with compassion and authenticity. It's about walking this life path as your truest self, flaws and all, and inspiring others to do the same.

So, I challenge you to embrace the possibility that it can be easy to be seen as an intuitive and heart-centered leader. Trust in your own innate wisdom and goodness, and know that you have everything you need within you to lead with grace and integrity.

With love and belief in your potential,
Yourself

Dear Me,

It's not often that I take the time to reflect on my own potential as a leader, especially one who leads with intuition and compassion. Your question has sparked something within me, a glimmer of recognition that perhaps it can be easier than I've allowed myself to believe.

As I sit with this idea, I realize that the difficulty doesn't lie in embodying the qualities of intuition and heart-centered leadership, but in trusting myself enough to fully embrace them. So often, I find myself doubting my instincts or second-guessing my decisions, afraid of making mistakes or being judged by others.

But what if it doesn't have to be that way? What if I could trust in my intuition and lead from the heart without fear or hesitation? What if I could show up authentically, fully embracing my strengths and vulnerabilities, and inspire others to do the same?

It's a liberating thought, and one that fills me with a sense of possibility and excitement. I know that it won't happen overnight, and that there will be challenges along the way. But I'm ready to embrace the journey, trusting in my own inner wisdom and allowing myself to be seen as the intuitive and heart-centered leader that I know I can be.

Thank you for reminding me of my potential and inspiring me to step into my power with courage and conviction. I'm grateful for your wisdom and guidance, and I look forward to seeing where this journey takes us.

With love and determination,
Me

Note to reader: Thank you for taking this journey with me. For more insights about living with wisdom, get my book bonus and learn more on Facebook: https://www.facebook.com/JaneSays85/

Month End Review

What was new, good, and different about this month?

_____
_____
_____
_____
_____
_____
_____
_____
_____
_____
_____
_____
_____
_____
_____
_____
_____
_____
_____
_____
_____
_____
_____

Energy Almanac 2025 Edition

Year End Review

◇◇◇

What was new, good, and different about this year?
What do I want to see manifest next year?

_____

_____

_____

_____

_____

_____

_____

_____

_____

_____

_____

_____

_____

_____

_____

_____

_____

_____

_____

WATCH FOR THE UPCOMING
IN YOUR JAMMIES YEAR-END REVIEW

GO TO CHOOSEBIGCHANGE.COM AND
SIGN UP FOR OUR NEWSLETTER TO STAY IN THE LOOP

Energy Almanac 2025 EDITION

♡ Love the Energy Almanac? Tag us on social media: @TheEnergyAlmanac ♡

DO YOU WANT TO KNOW
What 2026 Will Bring?

ORDER THE NEW
Energy Almanac
FOR 2026, TODAY!

Go to: **https://choosebigchange.com**

Tell a friend, too!

GET OTHER INCREDIBLE PRODUCTS TO MAKE YOUR TRANSFORMATION FAST, FUN, AND EASY!

✵ https://choosebigchange.com ✵

Energy Almanac 2025 EDITION

Made in the USA
Coppell, TX
11 February 2025

45795507R00103